SAY IT!

The Odyssey of Clyde the Camel
is based on a trip that the author took in 2014. It is part travelogue and part fantasy. Just about everything in the book is true with some "poetic license" taken.

The story is told through the eyes of a stuffed camel that Nachin acquired on her journey. Clyde is naïve in the ways of the world but gains deep insights into human nature while accompanying the group of travelers. This story conveys Nachin's philosophy that one should try and find the humor in every challenging situation. She hopes that people of all ages will find the story entertaining as well as informative.

Also by Sarah J. Nachin

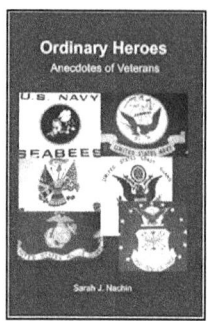 

ORDINARY HEROES, ANECDOTES OF VETERANS

ORDINARY HEROES relate, in their own words, the experiences of men and women who served in the American military forces through five decades of conflict. These stories - humorous, heartwarming, tragic and gripping - are a testimony to the unconquerable human spirit.

THE LONG JOURNEY
with Felicia McCranie

THE LONG JOURNEY is the story of how one woman was saved from despair and self-destruction – the lowest place a person can be. She is now an ordained minister and shares her story to help other people find meaning and joy in their lives.

Both books are available on Amazon

The Odyssey of Clyde the Camel

by
Sarah J. Nachin

Copyright © 2018 Sarah J. Nachin

All rights reserved. Except for the inclusion of brief quotations in a review, no part of this book may be reproduced in any form without permission in writing from the author or publisher.

Published in the USA
ISBN 978-1-57550-125-3

Printed in the United States of America
Book Design by Johanna M Bolton
Cover Art by Sarah & Lisah Scott
First Printing April 2018

Dedication

This book is dedicated to M.J., my mum. Without her I would not have written this story in the first place.

Acknowledgments

I'm grateful to Sarah Nachin who helped me put all my experiences down on paper.

It was Sarah's BFF, Myra Stack, that "planted the seeds" and inspired this book. She's been Sarah's best friend and confidant for almost thirty years.

My thanks to Jason and Julie. Many episodes in this book would not have happened if it hadn't been for them. They gave me a lot of insight into American teenagers.

I would like to thank Sarah's sister, Karen Sayko. She helped interpret some of the British sayings so that non-Brits would understand what I was saying. It's very true that England and America are two countries divided by a common language.

My new friend, Janet Ward, made sure that the French dialogue was translated properly into English. She's British, like me, but speaks French fluently. She's a world traveler and maybe one day I'll get to go on a trip with her.

Lynne Mueller-Nissen, a noted author, was an enormous aid in writing this book. She helped Sarah "find her voice." Jerry Cowling, another published author, helped edit this book and gave invaluable suggestions.

The beautiful sketch is the work of Patricia Miller of Spring Hill, Florida. Sarah and Lisah Scott designed the covers.

Table of Contents

- 1 - Prologue - A New Home
- 3 - Chapter 1 - The Yanks "Invade" Europe
- 8 - Chapter 2 - Cornwall, England
- 12 - Chapter 3 - Off to See the World
- 26 - Chapter 4 - The East Coast of England
- 36 - Chapter 5 - On to "Gay Paree"
- 53 - Chapter 6 - Meeting New Friends
- 59 - Chapter 7 – Misadventures
- 68 - Chapter 8 - Discovering New Places
- 78 - Chapter 9 - Andorra & the Cirque du Soleil
- 84 - Chapter 10 - Olé for Barcelona
- 96 - Chapter 11 - "Home" at Last
- 99 - Epilogue - How this Story Came to Be
- 101 - The Ballad of Clyde, the Camel
- 104 - Clyde's Scrapbook
- 115 - British English/American English Dictionary
- 117 - Index of People, Places & Things
- 122 - About the Author

"A journey is best measured in friends, rather than miles."
– Tim Cahill

"Trust in God, but tie your camel."
– Arab proverb

The Odyssey of Clyde the Camel

Prologue
A New Home

I was just a dusty, disheveled ordinary dromedary when a lady called M.J. found me in the New Curiosity Shop in *Cornwall*, England. I thought I was doomed to live out my days on a glass shelf, never to go anywhere or see anything; to be over-looked by dozens of people because I wasn't handsome like some of my other friends. The gingham dog and the calico cat were much more attractive than me. They had joined me on the shelf recently and we were already good friends. Andy Panda, Snowflake, and Fergus MacPherson were some of my other chums.

M.J. picked me up. I felt a ping of excitement. She dusted me off and inspected my partly torn ear, then reshaped my hump in her gentle hands. I hoped that this was a sign that my life was going to get better, much better than being "boy-handled" most of your life by a spoiled brat who would dump you in a toy chest underneath Legos, model cars, and dirty underwear.

After Ian, my bratty former owner, went off to prep

school his mum threw me in a box with all his other toys and dropped me off at the New Curiosity Shop, a charity shop. I've called it "home" for the past five years. It sucked!

When M.J. bought me it was the happiest day of my life. She loved animals (real and stuffed) and her soothing voice spoke about the numerous pets she had at home in America. I immediately thought of her as my mum. I never knew my real one, you know.

Just departing from the shelf, leaving my "prison" behind and finding a real home would have been enough for me. But, little did I know that this would be the start of my many adventures. I'd be meeting a lot of people and seeing many different places. Hey, this was going to be an adventure: The Odyssey of Clyde the Camel!

First, let me bring you "up to speed" about how I met M.J. and her friends. She told me all about how they came to be in this remote area of England.

Chapter 1
The Yanks "Invade" Europe

The sun was shining on a warm Florida day in February when Sally, M.J.'s friend, decided to take a trip to Europe. She had been overseas several times before and was looking forward to seeing friends there and taking in the sights. It required a lot of planning, especially when her 15-year-old grandson, Jason, and 13-year-old granddaughter, Julie, would be traveling with her.

Whilst planning her excursion, she phoned M.J. to talk about it. All of a sudden she came up with a brilliant idea.

"M.J., why don't you come to Europe with me?" she blurted out.

"I can only get a week off and besides I couldn't possibly afford it," M.J. replied, sadly.

"Well, just come for a week, then. We'll be staying in Cornwall and London for a week and then continue on our trip."

"That just might work! Let me see if I can schedule my vacation to coincide with your trip. When are you going?"

"We'll be leaving the first week of June as soon as the kids get out of school."

M.J. was able to get the time off and Sally immediately booked their flights and hotels with her friend, Judi, the owner of a travel agency called *Take Time for Travel*. Sally, M.J., Julie and Jason became more excited as the time for their departure neared.

When the big day finally arrived, an entourage was at the airport to wish them "Bon Voyage." You would have thought they were rock stars. A horde of family and friends gathered to say good-bye to the world travelers. This was the start of their five-week trip, taking them to four different countries.

The foursome boarded the jumbo jet and settled into their seats for the first leg of their flight. When the plane touched down in Philadelphia for a two-hour layover, they were eager to stretch their legs and get a bite to eat.

"Julie, Jason, wait up for us," Sally said, as the two teenagers plowed ahead.

"You guys are walking too slow," Jason replied. "I'm hungry."

"Yeah, me too," said Julie.

They found a food court and ate their over-priced sandwiches. After the kids gobbled down their meal, they immediately disappeared to locate a "hot spot" for their smart phones. Sally settled in to rest whilst M.J. explored the terminal. Before long, they heard the announcement for their connecting flight and got in the queue to board the plane.

"It's going to be a long night and a long flight, so you might as well settle in and rest, guys." Sally advised.

The excitement of traveling kept Sally awake so she decided to watch a film. She looked over at her two charges and couldn't tell if they were asleep. The glare from the screens on their mobiles illuminated their transfixed eyes and they appeared comatose. At some point Sally dozed off, but it seemed she had only been asleep for a short time when she heard the captain's voice.

"Ladies and gentlemen please observe the fasten seat belt signs whilst we prepare for landing at Heathrow. The weather is beautiful, and we should be touching down at approximately 9:00 a.m. local time. Thank you for flying with us."

People in the cabin began to stir. M.J and Sally peered out of the window and watched as the trees, buildings and cars grew larger and larger. Jason and Julie gradually woke up and stretched.

"Yay! We're finally here!" Julie exclaimed.

"Now, everyone, we have to stick together," Sally stated emphatically, as they disembarked. "This isn't Philly."

They entered the terminal and searched for customs. As they waited in the queue, Sally got out the passports that had been safely tucked away in the pouch tied around her waist. Julie was with M.J. in one queue and Jason was in front of Sally in the other.

When they got to the front, the customs agent

checked Julie and M.J.'s passports and waved them through. When it was Sally's turn the agent queried her.

Pointing to Jason, he asked, "Madam, is this young man with you?"

"Yes, sir. He's my grandson. I have signed permission from his parents for him to travel with me."

"Your documents, Madam," he said in a stern voice.

"They're in my suitcase that's with the checked baggage."

"Then we have a problem, Madam."

Sally's heart began to pound.

"I have copies of their birth certificates and signed papers from their parents."

"But you don't have them with you at the present. Is that correct?"

Sally glanced at Jason as he turned around and saw what looked like a smirk on his face. She was starting to get very nervous.

"But, sir..."

"Well, Madam, I could make you wait until your luggage goes through customs, but I won't."

"Thank you very much, sir. I really appreciate your understanding."

Sally and Jason quickly passed through the gate before the agent had a chance to change his mind and caught up with the others.

"Wow, Grandma. That sure was funny. That guy must have thought you were trying to kidnap me."

"YOU THINK IT WAS FUNNY!?"

They picked up their luggage from the carousel and

then proceeded to look for signs telling how to get to the train station. M.J. came to the rescue because Sally was "brain-dead" from lack of sleep.

They finally located the place where the shuttle would take them into London, bought their tickets and boarded the bus. Soon they were at *Paddington Station*. Sally purchased the *Brit Rail Passes* and the group waited for the next train to Cornwall. (I found out much later that there is a popular book about a stuffed bear called Paddington. Maybe I'll get to be famous like him one day.)

Paddington Station

Chapter 2
Cornwall, England

Now, this is where I come in.

Cornwall is a picturesque region on the west coast of England. It's rumoured that King Arthur's castle is there. You can visit Tintagel and see the ruins of that ancient fortress.

Sally liked to watch *Doc Martin* on the telly, just like the lady who owned The New Curiosity Shop, so most of the sights were familiar to her. Even the people seemed to have stepped right out of that programme.

M.J. liked to shop at charity shops, so when she spotted the sign outside my home she had to stop in and investigate.

"Look at all the cool stuff!" she exclaimed to Sally.

"Just like we have in Florida," Sally replied nonchalantly.

"What an adorable little camel," M.J. said, as she

picked me up. "You are definitely coming home with me."

My heart skipped a beat.

"I even have a name for you – Clyde, after the camel in the song 'Ahab, the Arab.'"

M.J. paid the proprietor and tucked me carefully into her tote bag. Just before she did, I looked back at my friends. I could see the sadness in their eyes, knowing that I would be leaving them. I felt a little sad too but happy that I would be finding a home with such a nice lady.

It was great being with so many real people after being stuck on a shelf with old clothes, smelly shoes, and cast-off junk. Oh, excuse me all you charity shop proprietors, cast-off "treasures."

I got to stay with the Americans in their cottage at the *Wheal Rodney Lodges* in *Marazion*. It was brilliant to sleep in a real bed for the first time in a long, long while.

The lodges were perfect for a family. There were two bedrooms, a loo, salon, telly, Wi-Fi. It even had a kitchen with a fridge and cooker. The humans could go swimming in an indoor pool. I don't swim – remember where I come from. We were just a short walk down a quiet country lane to the center of town.

The teenagers shared one bedroom because they liked to stay up late. The adults shared the other. At least that was the way it was supposed to be. M.J. told me that the first night they stayed there she ended up sleeping on the fold-out couch in the salon because Sally's snoring kept her awake.

Jason and Julie liked to listen to music on their mobiles and chat with their friends on Facebook. Sally liked to talk to everyone and take lots of pictures and videos. Mum made sure I was taken care of and that I was included in all their activities. She hardly left me alone for one minute.

I'm really glad it was M.J. that adopted me because Sally seemed to have a knack for losing things or forgetting where she put them. I guess she's like my friend, Ellen the elephant. Despite what you've heard, not all elephants have good memories.

One day we went to *St. Michael's Mount*, a small island that is home to a castle dating back to the 12th century. We were able to walk over on a brick path at low tide and spent about two hours exploring the grounds, taking in the fantastic views and going through the castle seeing all kinds of cool stuff, like coats of armor.

Well, we almost got stranded because by the time we were done, the tide was coming in and the water was up to the humans' knees. I'm just glad Mum was carrying me because, like I said before, I can't swim. It was much harder going back to the mainland than it was going out. After about twenty minutes of wading through the water and watching with horror as it got higher and higher, we were back on dry land. Actually, we wouldn't have been stranded, even if the water had come all the way up to the humans' chins, because there is a ferry that runs back and forth. I just wanted to say that to add some excitement to my story (Ha! Ha!). After our adventures at St. Michael's Mount we stopped at the *Fire Engine Inn* for some *Cornish pasties*. Be sure you pronounce it properly. It's a Short "A," not a Long "A." That's another thing all together – not very edible.

The proprietor, Trevor, was a jolly good chap and kept the Yanks entertained with jokes and stories. The food was delicious too, at least that's what the humans kept saying.

Clyde in Penzance

Chapter 3
Off to See the World

After three days, we left Marazion and took a taxi to *Penzance* where we would catch the train back to London. I had learned all about Penzance from a pirate doll I had met at the New Curiosity Shop. He had played a part in *The Pirates of Penzance*. Or so he told me.

I was on my way to see the great big world and my very first train ride! How brilliant was that!

The conductors were nice. They came 'round and checked to make sure everyone had a ticket and were on the right train. Sometimes they used a machine to check the tickets and sometimes they punched it by hand – like you see in the old films. I guess M.J. was kind of naughty. She hid me in her bag when the conductor came around because I didn't have a ticket.

"Tickets are only for people, Clyde," she explained.

"You're a stow-away, Clyde," Sally joked, making it sound more exciting.

The Odyssey of Clyde the Camel

When we arrived in London, we got a taxi to take us to our hotel. The Americans had so much luggage we had to get an extra-large cab. I'm glad I'm a camel and don't need luggage because it looked like it was really hard for them to manage all their suitcases and backpacks. I noticed other people around us were only carrying one suitcase and some only had a backpack. Heck, I don't even need a water bottle because I carry my water in my hump. Talk about traveling light!

Our hotel was called *Bayswater Inn* and was located in a fancy part of town near *Hyde Park* and *Kensington Gardens*. The nice man at reception gave my humans the room keys and showed us the way to the lift.

As soon as we were settled in we headed out to explore. Jason and Julie wanted to eat and buy tacky souvenirs. Sally wanted to look at sights and take pictures (of course). I think M.J. just wanted to rest, but she followed along like a real soldier.

We ate dinner at – where else – McDonald's.

"This is the biggest McDonald's, I've ever seen," said Julie.

"Two levels!" said Jason as he rushed to be first in line and first to get his food.

"I'll go find a table downstairs," he offered.

"No. We all need to stick together," Sally responded.

"Aw. C'mon, Grandma. I'm not a baby."

"You heard me!" Sally said, raising her voice ever so slightly to get her point across.

After dinner and a little shopping, we headed back to the hotel. I wasn't tired at all, but the rest of the group were exhausted and were soon asleep. Well, all except for "Tweedledee" and "Tweedledum." (That was what Mum had started calling them.) They stayed up most of the night listening to tunes on their mobiles. The next morning Sally was the first to wake up. She knocked on our door.

"Are you awake?"

"I am now," Mum answered groggily.

"I'm going down for breakfast. Do you wanna come?"

"Yes. Give me about ten minutes. Are Jason and Julie coming?"

"Are you kidding me? I think they're dead; they're sleeping so soundly."

A few minutes later we headed for the lift.

"The breakfast room is on the first floor," Sally said, pressing the button marked 1.

When the lift stopped, Mum got out and surveyed the area.

"This doesn't look like the lobby," she remarked.

I could have told them that in England, the first floor is called the ground floor and the second floor is actually the first floor. Confusing, I know. I *would* have told my humans, but I'm afraid that if I had said anything it would have really freaked them out. (See, I've picked up American slang.)

"This food looks really good," Sally said, after figuring out the lift and arriving at the dining area.

"I guess so," replied M.J. "But whoever heard of baked beans for breakfast?"

After eating, we went back to our rooms and Sally shook the kids until they woke up.

"Quit it, Grandma!" Julie yelled.

"Rise and shine, sleepy heads."

"Uhh, what time is it?" Jason groaned.

"It's 8:15. We need to get going."

"8:15!" Julie remarked incredulously. "At home, Mom lets us sleep as late as we want."

"Well, we're not home and I'm not Mom. Let's get going."

"Okay. Okay. But we have to have something to eat first," Jason lamented.

"Breakfast is still being served downstairs."

"All right. We'll be ready in a few minutes," said Julie.

Well, I don't know how long a few minutes is in America, but by 9:00, the pair were finally ready to leave after Julie's extensive preparations of fixing her hair and putting on her makeup and Jason's time in the bathroom washing his face, brushing his teeth, combing his hair and deciding which pair of sneakers to put on. We went back downstairs and entered the breakfast area.

"This food looks gross," remarked Jason.

"Yuck! Baked beans, grilled tomatoes," added Julie.

"Fine. Have a food bar," said Sally.

Our merry band of travelers set out for the Underground. When we descended the stairs to get on the tube, we were confronted by a massive throng of people and a confusing assortment of signs.

"How the heck do we figure this out?" Sally

inquired.

"Okay. We need to get to Charing Cross Road to pick up the *London Passes* that you ordered while we were in Philly. The signs say take the blue line to this stop, then transfer to the red line, then transfer again here and that will take us to Charing Cross," M.J. instructed after studying the map on the wall for a couple of minutes.

Sally's jaw dropped. Even Tweedledee and Tweedledum seemed impressed.

"You're good, M.J. I would never have been able to make any sense of this."

We all had fun riding the tube and we were very careful to "mind the gap." This was a warning that comes over the loud speakers every time you get on and off. I was sure lucky that M.J. had me tucked safely in her tote bag because "the gap" was bigger than me.

When we got to the ticket kiosk, Sally gave the man everyone's names so each human could have their very own pass. These would give us unlimited rides on the tube and buses, discounts for attractions, maps and all kinds of other good stuff. They even put the pass in plastic and put it on a cord to hang around your neck. I wish I could have had one.

Sally thought it would be neat to see a show at the *West End*. The group decided on *Stomp*, so she bought discounted tickets for that evening.

Our first stop was the *British Museum*. The humans decided to split up because everyone had different ideas about what they wanted to see.

Clyde with a London Pass

"You guys will be sticking with me," Sally said to the kids.

"No way, Grandma," Jason and Julie said in unison.

"We don't want to spend all day looking at mummies, broken pieces of pottery and other junk," Julie complained.

"It's not going to be all day. It will only be a couple

of hours."

"I want to go back to the hotel," Jason whined.

"Okay, listen. You guys can go on your own, but don't leave the building, don't touch anything, be polite to people and meet us at the coffee shop at noon – not a minute later."

"What do you think we are, Grandma? A couple of hoodlums?" Julie queried.

"She refuses to answer that question on the grounds that she's a Girl Scout and never tells a lie," M.J. joked.

Everyone burst out laughing.

I thought the New Curiosity Shop had a lot of neat old stuff, but the British Museum was brilliant. Everything you can imagine was there. From prehistoric times to the Twentieth Century. I think my favorite was the *Rosetta Stone*. I don't mean the language learning program. It's a large ancient rock with symbols etched into it. Discovered in 1799, it actually dates back to 196 BC and provided the key to understanding Egyptian hieroglyphics.

Our next stop was *Harrods Department Store*. It's the most famous store in the world. They say you can buy anything from a yacht to a bag of candy there. Sally wanted to visit Harrods because her mum had worked there and she had heard a lot about it. The store was HUGE. We walked around and Sally even chatted with the salesmen in the men's department. That's where her mum had worked.

After Harrods we went to *#10 Downing Street*, where our prime minister lives and we also saw the guards at *Buckingham Palace*.

"God Save our gracious Queen, long live our noble Queen, God save the Queen!"

Oh, so sorry. I got carried away.

"We're going to visit the *National Portrait Gallery* next," Sally said.

"Not another stupid museum!" Julie moaned.

"Yes, another stupid museum," M.J. retorted sarcastically.

The National Portrait Gallery had a gazillion pictures in it. Kings, queens and other famous people. It seemed like we saw every single one. This time it was M.J. who took lots of pictures. Maybe one day, I'll have my portrait hanging there.

After a long day of walking many blocks and riding miles on the tube we headed back to the hotel.

We had a quick bite to eat and then it was time to get ready to go to the *Ambassadors Theatre* in the West End to see *Stomp*. When I heard we were going to the theatre, I thought we were going to see a film. I really wanted to see *Lawrence of Arabia*. An old camel at the New Curiosity Shop told me he had actually met T.E. Lawrence. I think he might have been "pulling my hump." He used to brag a lot.

Stomp turned out to be the "bee's knees." All the humans enjoyed the show, too, even Jason who didn't like a lot of things and was hard to impress.

One of my old friends, a wise owl called Orville, had told me that plays and books are supposed to have something called a "plot." I think the plot of this show was: "Even if your parents tell you that you shouldn't make a lot of noise banging on garbage cans, it's okay because it's lots of fun and people really like it."

When we got back to the hotel, Sally gave Jason and Julie strict orders.

"No staying up late! We have an early train to catch for *Stonehenge* in the morning."

I had seen a picture book about Stonehenge at the New Curiosity Shop. I couldn't figure out why a bunch of rocks standing on end was such a big deal.

The next morning everyone was up bright and early - quite a feat for Jason and Julie who weren't used to getting up before the crack of noon. Sorry, that was a bit sarcastic.

We rode the train to the town of *Salisbury* and then got on the bus that took us to Stonehenge. I must admit for a weird bunch of rocks, it was pretty ace. The humans put on headsets attached to a little box. A voice came out of the box telling all about the monument.

Archaeologists believe that the rocks were put in place by primitive people between 3,000 and 2,000 BC. It must have taken a long time for them to do it since they didn't have bulldozers or any kind of machinery to move the rocks. Nobody knows for sure why they did it. I guess with no TV or Internet, they had to do something to keep from getting bored. Some people think it might have been a burial ground or a sort of church where religious ceremonies were held or a place where people went to be healed. It could have even been a place where human sacrifices were made. Yuck! The most accepted theory is that it was a sort of observatory or calendar where people could look at the sky and even make predictions about eclipses. Brilliant!

We rode the bus back to town and had lunch. Then we started walking towards *Salisbury Cathedral*, but before we got there M.J. spied a charity shop.

"Let's stop in here and look around," she suggested.

"Good idea, I want to sit down and rest," Julie said.

"You mean you're tired already. We've hardly walked three blocks," said Sally.

Julie gave her a look that only a teenage girl can give.

While M.J. and Sally went inside, Jason and Julie sat down on the curb and simultaneously pulled out their mobiles.

"Don't move from this spot," Sally warned.

The shop was very similar to my old home, full of all kinds of interesting objects. Mum started trying on hats and Sally was looking through old books.

Soon, Sally said, "I'm going to start walking on ahead. I'll meet you at the cathedral."

She went outside and found Julie and Jason still sitting in the same spot.

"I'm going now. Come along."

The two seemed not to hear.

"I said 'Come on'," she repeated.

"Okay, Grandma," Julie said, her eyes transfixed on her mobile.

"Listen, if you want to stay here and wait for M.J., that's fine with me."

"Okay, Grandma," Jason replied mechanically.

Sally walked slowly down the street taking in the sights. About fifteen minutes later we caught up with her.

"Where are Jason and Julie?" Sally asked.

"I thought they were with you," M.J. replied.

"I left them at the store and told them to come with you. Oh my God!"

Just then her phone rang.

"Who the heck could be calling me?"

She pressed the button and the voice on the other end said, "Hi, Sally. This is Sharon."

It was the children's mother calling from America.

"Jason just texted me. He said you left them behind." The sound of panic in her voice.

"No, I didn't. I told them to stay at the store and come with M.J. Okay, we'll just retrace our steps. They couldn't be far."

"How's everything going?" Sharon asked.

"Oh, just wonderful."

"I'm glad to hear that," Sharon replied, not recognizing the sarcasm in Sally's tone.

"Did Jason say where they were?"

"Yes. They're waiting near the shop."

"Well, good. At least they didn't wander off. We'll go back and get them," Sally said, half wishing that she could just abandon them.

The four were soon reunited.

"I'm glad you stayed close by so we could find you," Sally told them. "That was the right thing to do."

"We keep telling you that we're not dumb little kids," Jason replied.

The Odyssey of Clyde the Camel

"I know that, but it's important to be aware of things and to follow my orders," Sally said, in a mock gruff tone.

"Yeah, yeah, yeah," Julie replied.

They proceeded on their way towards the cathedral, with Julie and Jason trudging three or four steps behind and Sally constantly looking over her shoulder to make sure that the wayward pair were still following.

Salisbury Cathedral is a large church dating back to the 13th Century. It has the tallest spire in all of England. There's also an original of the *Magna Carta*. Now, I don't speak Latin, but what that means in English is "Great Charter." It was written in 1215 and is an important symbol of liberty. They wrote it on parchment sheets using quill pens made from feathers since they didn't have computers, typewriters or paper. Those poor birds. It must have hurt when they pulled out the feathers!

The next day would be our last in London, so Sally and M.J. decided to take a tour of the city on a double-decker bus. Julie was excited about the prospect, but Jason wasn't impressed.

"Can I stay here? I'm really tired."

"Okay, but you're not leaving the hotel," Sally replied.

"WHAT!!" Jason exclaimed.

"I don't want you wandering around London by yourself and I'll tell the man at the front desk that if he sees you try to leave, he has my permission to stop you or tell me when I get back."

"Aw, C'mon! That's not fair."

"I don't care. You either come with us or stay here

at the hotel. I'll leave a sandwich and some drinks for you. You can go anywhere in the hotel, but you're not to step foot outside."

"That sucks," Jason lamented.

"We'll only be gone for a few hours. We'll be back before supper. You can watch TV, listen to your tunes or chat with your friends on Facebook."

The four of us departed leaving Jason still muttering under his breath. We rode the tube to the place where we were to catch the bus. Sally had booked us a tour with a theme. It was like "Back to the Future." The tour guide was dressed in costume and we pretended like we were going back in time to visit famous places and even hear famous people like William Shakespeare and Henry VIII speak to us. It was jolly good fun!!

The bus took us around *Piccadilly Circus*. Some circus! There weren't even any animals or acrobats. Then we rode over London Bridge. I was kind of afraid it would fall down. We even went past the *Tower of London* where they kept the prisoners before they were beheaded. Cool! The guards there are called Beefeaters. I don't know what else they eat. The last stop was *Trafalgar Square* which wasn't even square.

"This was a really neat tour," Julie said as we got off the bus. "Jason is going to be sorry he missed it."

The next day it was time for M.J. to return to her home in Florida and for the others to continue their trip. Mum had to go back to something called "work." From her tone of voice in describing it, "work" didn't sound like half as much fun as "holiday."

"Would you like to keep Clyde with you?" she asked Sally. "Kind of like a mascot."

"That would be cool. I'll take good care of him"

Panic and horror came over me. My mum leaving me! I felt something wet around my eyes and remembered the same thing happening when my first human's mother had dropped me off at the charity shop. I was crying!

"Look, I've gone and spilled water on Clyde!" M.J. exclaimed.

I didn't want her to leave me. What if Sally lost me somewhere? Then I'd never get to see America.

As Sally and M.J. were talking, I noticed Jason and Julie rolling their eyes. I don't think they liked me.

"Talk about lame," Jason scoffed.

"Yeah," Julie chimed in.

M.J. placed me carefully in Sally's tote bag.

"Take good care of Clyde and take lots of pictures with him. Okay," she said.

"Don't worry. I will."

Chapter 4
The East Coast of England

We checked out of the hotel, took a taxi to the train station and boarded the train for *Felixstowe*. Sally's mother had been born in the small seaside town and grew up there. When she was a little girl, Sally had lived nearby. She wanted to visit her mum's friends in the town and see if the place had changed in all those years.

When we got to Felixstowe we caught a cab to the *Marlborough Hotel,* located right across from the beach. Sally went to reception to register and we then went up to our rooms on a really, really small lift with an iron cage around it like the old-fashioned ones you see in the classic films.

We had a suite with colour telly in each room, a phone and a loo (of course). Not something I have to worry about but very important to humans.

Once we settled in, it was time to go exploring. First stop – the beach.

"Hey, Jason. I bet you don't know what this body of water is called." said Sally.

"The Atlantic Ocean?"

"Nope."

"I know. It's the English Channel," Julie piped up.

"Wrong, again, but we'll be seeing that soon."

"Just tell us, Grandma. Stop acting like a schoolteacher," Jason joked.

"It's the North Sea."

"Does that mean there's a South Sea, West Sea and East Sea?" Julie asked, half-kiddingly.

"I don't know. Why don't you look it up on the Internet?"

"Yeah, RI…GHT. SU…RE. Like I'm gonna do that," replied Jason.

"This isn't anything like our beaches in Florida. The sand is a different colour and it's mostly real little stones instead of fine grains of sand," Julie observed.

"And look at all these big rocks and boulders. We don't have those on our beaches. This is really cool," Jason added.

The two began to race each other to the closest group of boulders and proceeded to scurry up the large rocks.

"Be careful, guys. I don't want to have to take you to the hospital with any broken bones."

Sally walked quietly along the beach as the kids waded in the water and wrote "Jason & Julie were here.

June 2014" in the sand. She was thinking back to the days when she was a little girl and would play on the beach with her older sister, Kathy. Sally looked happy and sad at the same time. Humans are rather strange.

The next day, Sally went on a long walk by herself. She had invited Jason and Julie to come with her.

"I'm too tired, Grandma," Julie moaned.

"Me too," Jason agreed. "Besides, we want to play pool in the lounge downstairs and go to the beach."

"Or are you going to keep us prisoners in the hotel like you did with Jason in London?" Julie inquired.

"No. You can go to the beach and even take a walk if you want to."

Sally knew that Felixstowe, being a small town, would be safe.

"Just don't get lost," she warned.

"Look who's talking." Julie chimed in.

Sally had told me that she didn't have the best sense of direction. She had once gotten lost in a town that only had two streets.

"Okay, don't be a wise guy," she kidded.

Map in hand, Sally grabbed her camera and started off to explore her mum's hometown. She could smell the crisp salt air and hear the chatter of the other people walking on the promenade. Everyone smiled at her and said, "Good Morning."

"I fancy a cuppa," she said to me. "Gosh, I'm starting to sound British."

She spied a café and went in.

"May I help you, Miss?" the grey-haired lady behind

the counter asked.

"Yes, please. I'd like a cup of tea. And do you have any scones?"

"Do I have any scones? Is the Archbishop of Canterbury Anglican?"

"That's a good one," Sally laughed.

"Comin' right up, Luv. You're American, aren't you?"

"How did you ever guess? But, my Mum was born and raised here. I'm on holiday with my grandchildren."

"How luvely. Is this your first trip to Felixstowe?"

"No. I was here when I was a child."

"So, has it changed much?"

"The beach is exactly as I remember it. The town has changed a bit, though. There weren't any Indian restaurants or pizza parlors when I was here before," Sally replied with a smile.

A few minutes later, the woman returned to Sally's table with a steaming pot of tea and a small china cup. Then she brought a small plate holding a warm scone and some butter, along with a tiny jar of orange marmalade.

"There you go, Luv. By the way, I'm called Margaret. What's your name?"

"I'm called Sally."

She was *really* starting to get the hang of this British English.

"Well, it's very nice to meet you, Sally."

"This is real tea," Sally remarked. "Not the kind that comes from a tea bag."

"Tea bags – what a sacrilege!"

"And the water is boiling hot. You just can't get a good cup of tea in a restaurant back home."

"Tsk,Tsk. You poor thing. How do you ever manage?"

I could tell by Margaret's tone of voice that she wasn't joking. We Brits take our tea very seriously and with a little milk and sugar. Okay, I guess that was kind of a lame joke.

After finishing her tea and scone, Sally said goodbye to Margaret, promising to come back again while she was in town. Continuing on her stroll, Sally was soon in the main shopping district. There were all sorts of businesses. Antiques, solicitors, estate agents. She even spied a tattoo parlor.

"I have to get a picture of this and send it to Joe," Sally remarked.

I found out later that Joe was a friend of Sally's who was a tattoo artist. I knew what they were because once a lady with pictures all over her body came into The New Curiosity Shop. She even picked me up and told me how cute I was. I thought for sure she was going to take me home with her, but she bought some vintage clothes instead. Maybe I'll get a tattoo one day.

Sally's next stop was the *Spa Pavilion*. It was a theatre where her auntie had performed as a singer in the 1930s and 1940s but was now closed down. The place looked abandoned. Then she spotted a man.

"Can I help you, Miss?"

"Yes. I was wondering if I could go in and look around. My aunt performed here many years ago."

The Odyssey of Clyde the Camel

"You don't say. Isn't that brilliant. My name's Roger. I'm the caretaker, so to speak. Sure, I'll be glad to take you 'round."

"Oh, thank you so much. My name's Sally."

"I used to be the stage manager here," said Roger as he led us inside the dusty lobby.

"Really. You must have some interesting stories to tell."

"Ah, don't get me started, now," he laughed.

"How long has the Spa Pavilion been here?" Sally inquired.

"It opened in 1909. Of course, I don't remember that," Roger said, chuckling at his own joke.

"Wow, you don't look that old," Sally replied, tongue firmly planted in cheek.

"Vitamins and clean leaving," the caretaker answered, laughing.

"And when did the theatre close?"

"Well, it was quite the place to go for over thirty years. Then the Jerrys dropped a bomb on it in 1941."

"Oh, my gosh. What a shame."

"Yes. It was a bloody tragedy. But, you know us Brits. Nothing keeps us down. 'Keep calm and carry on' and all that. We re-built it from the ground up and the old girl was back in business in 1950."

"Why did it close?"

"It was going strong until the 1990s. But I think the younger generation was too interested in telly, cinema and rock concerts to want to see something as old-fashioned as musical theatre. It finally closed for good in

2013."

"So what's going to happen with it now?"

"Well, that's the good news. The town council is helping a group of citizens raise money to re-open the Spa. We hope to have it up and running by next year."

"That's fantastic! Maybe I'll get to come back and see a show."

"You must do that. For your auntie's sake."

"I really appreciate you showing me around. You made my day."

"It was a pleasure. Now, I must get back to work. I'll tell you an old saying to remember me by. 'Old stage managers never die. They just keep standing by.' "

"That's a good one."

"Well, do come back and bring your friend," Roger said, pointing to me.

Did that ever give me a thrill! Maybe they'll do a production of *Desert Song*.

The next day, Annie, a friend of Sally's, met us at the hotel. Actually, she was the daughter of Sally's mum's best friend. Annie had lived in Felixstowe all her life. Sally hadn't seen Annie for over fifty years. Gosh, I'm not even that old.

Annie picked us up in her car and took all of us on a tour of Felixstowe. She showed Sally where her mum had grown up and where Sally's grandfather had worked - the Felix Hotel. It was now a home for old-age pensioners. Then we all went to Annie's house for tea and sandwiches. A lot of Annie's family were there - her husband, Albert; her two brothers, Ronald and Bertram;

her 100-year-old father, Peter and her aunt, Clara.

Everyone was so welcoming. The years that had passed since Sally had last seen them just melted away like ice cream on a hot summer day. They talked about old times and looked at family photographs. Annie served the most delicious sandwiches. Well, at least they looked delicious. No one offered me any.

When it was time to leave, Ronald was nice enough to offer to take us the next day to *Horham*, the air base where Sally's father had been stationed during World War II. That sounded like jolly good fun.

Promptly at 8:00 a.m. Ronald drove up to the Marlborough in his classic *Morris Mini*. We drove the thirty miles to *Eye* where Horham is located. Sally's dad had flown with the 95th Bomb Group on a B-17 during the war.

Horham Army Air Base

The townspeople, as a way of honoring the brave men of the 95th, had restored the airbase so that it looked as it had more than seventy years ago. They had even turned one of the quonset huts into a museum.

A very nice gentleman called James Mutton met us there and showed us 'round. I must say, it was quite interesting. Julie and Jason even got into the spirit.

"This is Charlie-Echo-Niner-Niner-Six. Do you read me? Over," Jason said, as he sat in a refurbished cockpit wearing a pair of authentic head phones.

"I read you loud and clear, Charlie-Echo-Niner-Niner-Six. You're cleared for takeoff on Runway 2-4-5. Over," Julie responded.

James took us into a big room where the townspeople hold dances.

"We dress up in 1940's clothing and dance to the music of the big bands. It's really a hoot."

Sally and the children bought some souvenirs and then said their goodbyes to James.

"Do you fancy a bite to eat?" Ronald asked.

"Yes. We're starved," Julie and Jason said in unison, before Sally could open her mouth.

"Sure. That sounds like a great idea. It'll be my treat."

The four stopped at a pub just down the road. Julie and Jason feasted on hamburgers and crisps. Sally ordered soup and a salad. Ronald ordered a Ploughman's Lunch.

"I need to make a stop before we head back to Felixstowe," Ronald said.

"Sure. We have all the time in the world," Sally

replied.

"I'm a beekeeper, you see, and I have to pick up some supplies from my friends just down the road. They raise grapes and make their own wine, too."

"Can we taste some?" Sally inquired, noticing the children's eyes light up.

"I don't see why not."

They soon arrived at their destination and were greeted by a smiling woman surrounded by several cats. Jason and Julie immediately went over and started playing with them.

"This is my friend, Sally and her two grands, Jason and Julie. Sally, this is Jenny Anderson. Where's Bill?"

"So nice to make your acquaintance. He's 'round back. Come on and I'll show you my grapes."

"Can we taste your wine?" Jason asked.

"Hush, Jason!" Sally said, throwing him a look that could kill.

"That's quite all right," Jenny laughed. "We don't check IDs here."

We walked through a field and came across rows and rows of the delicious fruit growing on vines. Each plant was labeled with the particular species.

"I didn't know there were so many different kinds of grapes," Sally observed.

We visited for a while with Jenny and Bill, Ronald picked up his supplies and soon we were headed back to Felixstowe.

Chapter 5
On to "Gay Paree"

The next morning we had to get up *very* early because we had so much to do. Well, at least the humans did. They finished packing, checked out and then caught the cab that Sally had booked the day before.

"Where are we headed for, Madam?" Jeffrey, the cabby, inquired.

"We need to catch the train for London and then from there we have to get the train to *Dover*. We're going to ride the ferry to *Calais*."

"You do realize that you have to get on the tube to go from one train station to the other?" Jeffrey asked.

"No, I didn't know that," Sally replied.

"That's going to be quite a feat with all your luggage."

"I know. But what other choice do we have?"

"Well, I can call my company and see if I can take

you to Dover."

"All that way. Won't it be kind of expensive?"

"I'll check and see."

After calling his office, Jeffrey gave Sally the price.

"That doesn't sound too bad considering everything. Let's do it!"

We were soon on the road out of town.

"Wait a second, we're going back to London. Can't we go straight from here to Dover?"

Clyde in the taxi

"We could, but it would take a lot longer. This way we can take the motorway and save a lot of time."

Sally whispered to me, "I hope he's not really 'taking us for a ride.'"

I guess she trusted Jeffrey because she didn't say anything to him.

We made good time until we got to London. Morning rush hour traffic.

While we sat in the gridlock, Sally took pictures and Jeffrey entertained us with all kinds of stories and jokes.

It wasn't too long before we were back on the motorway. The rest of the ride we zipped along at 110 kilometers per hour and before we knew it, the *White Cliffs of Dover* were in sight. In case you're thinking that we were riding with Mario Andretti or Jeff Gordon, let me explain. That's only 68 miles per hour.

The White Cliffs of Dover are awesome! They are made from chalk and are over two million years old. That's even older than my friend, Stanley, the stegosaurus!

We said ta-ta to Jeffrey as he dropped us off and helped us unload the bags. We were on our way to France!

The ferry was a really HUGE boat. It had a deck where you could sit and watch the coast of England as it faded into the distance.

"There's a telescope!" Julie exclaimed as she went over to get a better look.

"Can we get any food on board?" Jason asked.

"I'm sure they have a place to eat," Sally replied.

"I'm going down below," Jason said.

"I'm hungry, too," Julie added.

"Okay, I'll meet you there in a few minutes."

Sally sat on the deck admiring the scenery and watching the other people as they settled in for the 90-

minute trip.

"You know, Clyde, I'm starved, too."

She descended the stairs and soon reached the dining room. It was a large cafeteria-style eatery. She quickly spied her grands at a table eating hamburgers and crisps.

Clyde and Julie on the Ferry

Before you could say "Jack Robinson" we were pulling into the port of Calais. The humans gathered all their belongings and we stepped off the ferry onto dry land.

It was just a short walk to the train station where Sally bought our tickets for the train to Paris. Soon we were on the TGV. It's a high-speed train that goes about 322 kilometers per hour. When you say it in miles per hour (201 mph) it still sounds scary! Even though we were going pretty fast, we could look out the window at the neat scenery and I didn't even get dizzy.

The train pulled into Gare du Nord (Station of the North) in Paris about two hours later. It was time to gather all our gear for the umpteenth time and make our way to the taxi stand.

Sally kept remarking, "I'll never bring this much luggage with me again. It's costing me an arm and a leg for cab fare!"

That really scared me. How was she going to walk or carry suitcases with just one arm and one leg?

A nice man picked us up in a large cab. He spoke English very well and kept talking to Sally about politics and the president of the United States. Sally just nodded her head and agreed with everything he said. I found out later that is what's called being diplomatic or "how to make sure that you don't get your cab driver upset with you."

We arrived at the hotel and the driver helped us with our bags. Sally said, "Merci" and "Au Revoir" and then went to reception to check in.

The *Classics Hotel Paris Bastille* was very nice. After the gang unpacked, it was time to eat and then do a little exploring. Everyone agreed that the Chinese restaurant they had spied down the street would be just the thing. And I was looking forward to crepes!

After eating, we took off on a walk. I couldn't believe it was still daylight at 8:30 in the evening. With map in hand, Sally started strolling down the avenue, Jason and Julie trailing a few steps behind. She could smell the aromas coming from the patisseries and hear the laughter of people sitting at tables in the sidewalk cafés. She waited for Jason and Julie to catch up.

"It says here on the map that the Rue de la Bastille is the next block. That's where the famous Bastille is located."

"What's the Bastille, Grandma?" Julie asked.

"It was the prison where they kept people during the French Revolution before they sent them to the guillotine to chop off their heads."

"Cool!" Jason remarked.

When they arrived at the Rue de la Bastille, they looked up and down the street, but didn't see any big buildings.

"That's strange. It says on the map it's right here."

She spied a young woman walking her dog.

"I'll ask her if she knows."

"Aw, C'mon Grandma. Don't embarrass us."

"Didn't you know that's part of my job description?"

Sally approached the woman.

"Bon-Soir, Mademoiselle. Ou est la Bastille? (*Good evening, Miss. Where is the Bastille*?)"

"La-bas (*Over there*)," she said, pointing to a tall monument.

"Mais, ou est le grand bâtiment? (*But, where is the big building*?)" Sally asked, making a picture of a building with her two hands.

She had told me that sign language always came in handy if you weren't sure someone could understand you.

The woman laughed.

"You are American, no?"

"I'm afraid so."

"No big building anymore. Just the monument."

"Oh, I see," Sally replied, trying not to show her disappointment.

"It is torn down many years ago."

"Quel dommage (*What a shame*)," Sally remarked.

"No, it's a good thing. Very bad place."

"Oh, yes. Of course. I agree."

By then, Jason and Julie were kneeling down petting the dog.

"I like your dog," Julie said.

"Thank you, Mademoiselle."

"Merci pour votre aide (*Thank you for your help*)," Sally said.

"De rien (*It's nothing*) Enjoy your visit in Paris. You have such nice children."

"If she only knew," Sally whispered, winking at me.

The next day Sally and the kids decided to visit the Eiffel Tower. No one can go to Paris without seeing this famous landmark. They walked to the Metro stop and were soon at their destination.

The Eiffel Tower is enormous. Bigger than anything I've ever seen before. It reminded me of an erector set I once saw at the New Curiosity Shop. There were scads of tourists around and a lot of people selling souvenirs and other stuff.

Jason spied a group of people standing around a man sitting on the ground. He had three nut shells and was moving them around in circles. Jason went over to investigate. Sally and Julie followed.

"Jason, that's the oldest con game in the book," Sally said. "It's called the Shell Game and it's rigged."

"Lemme just take a look, Grandma," Jason protested.

The man placed a pea under one of the shells and started moving the shells around. Jason kept his eye on the one that hid the pea. Then the man stopped moving the shells.

"Ten Euros. Who know where is the pea?" he said in broken English.

A woman handed him a ten euro note and pointed to one of the shells. The man lifted the shell and, voilà, there was the pea.

"Very good, Madame. You win."

He handed the woman back her money and gave her another ten Euro note.

"I can do it, Grandma! I'm gonna play," Jason exclaimed.

"I wouldn't do it, if I were you. It's rigged. But it's your money if you wanna waste it."

Jason handed the man his money and watched carefully as the shells moved around in circles and then stopped.

"That one," Jason said, pointing to the shell in the middle.

No pea.

"Oh, crap," Jason said. "I was so sure. I watched very carefully."

"I told you so," Sally remarked, trying not to smile.

"This is boring," Julie said. "Let's go take some

more pictures of the Eiffel Tower."

As they were leaving the plaza, Jason spied another man playing the same game.

"I'm gonna go win my money back," Jason stated. "I think I've figured this game out."

"I don't think that's a good idea," Sally remarked.

"I can win. That lady won."

"Don't you know she's in on the scam?" Sally replied.

Nothing could deter Jason, so he went over to the other man, watched a few games and then handed the man his money.

It was "déjà vu all over again," as Yogi Berra used to say. I learned that phrase from Sally.

Not wanting to rub Jason's sad mistake in, Sally said, "Let's go see some other sights."

The four of us continued on our walk and soon arrived at the river Seine. We saw house boats moored on the banks and some motoring down the river. People were sitting on the grass relaxing and there were couples kissing. It looked like fun. Maybe I'll meet a cute lady camel one day. We also noticed a group of men setting up amplifiers and other equipment.

"What are these for?" Sally asked one of the workmen.

"We are having a dance later," he responded.

"That sounds like fun," Sally remarked.

As the afternoon wore on, Sally heard the usual comments from Julie and Jason: "*We're hungry. We're tired.*" So they walked to the Metro stop and went back to the neighborhood that was becoming very familiar to them.

"So, what do you guys want to eat?" Sally asked.

"Hamburgers," Jason replied.

"How about we get sandwiches from the shop down the street?"

They walked to the corner store and placed their orders. When the sandwiches were ready, we returned to the hotel to eat.

"I'm going back to the park in a little while to check out the dance," Sally said. "Do you wanna come?"

"Nah, that's okay. I'll stay here," Jason replied.

"Do you wanna come, Julie?"

"No. I'm tired."

"Okay. Well, I'll see you guys later. C'mon, Clyde."

Sally left the room, glancing back to see Tweedledee and Tweedledum with their faces glued to their mobiles.

We got on the Metro and were soon near the park. A crowd was already gathering and we could hear music playing.

There were people of all ages dancing to rock and roll music. Old and young were enjoying the fun. Sally watched, her feet keeping time to the music. An hour later, the sun was beginning to get low in the sky. It was a beautiful orange-red colour.

"Well, I think we'd better start heading home. It's a long way back to the Metro stop and my feet are getting tired," Sally said.

Sally walked hurriedly and I could tell her feet really were aching by the way she kept stopping and saying

"Ouch."

When we got to our stop, we got off and started walking toward the hotel.

I don't think we're going the right way, I thought.

"I don't think I'm going the right way," Sally said a few minutes later. "This doesn't look familiar. Shoot, I don't have my map with me, either. I'd better stop and ask for directions."

Sally spotted a well-dressed middle-aged woman coming out of a theatre.

"Ou est Le Classics Hotel, s'il vous plait. La rue de Charonne. (*Where is the Classics Hotel, please? Charonne Street*)," she inquired.

"Ah, Rue de Charonne," the woman replied.

She pointed a couple of times and said some words that I didn't know, but Sally seemed to understand.

We started out in the direction the woman had pointed in, made a couple of turns and were right back where we began. By now it was starting to get dark.

"Oh, brother. I'll never hear the end of it from the kids if they know I've gotten lost," Sally exclaimed.

I admit, I was starting to get a little worried. We walked down the wide avenue and then Sally spotted a hotel.

"I'm going to walk over there and see if the person at the front desk can give me good directions."

We were soon inside the well-lit hotel lobby. The nice young man at the front desk gave Sally good, clear directions and in less than ten minutes we were at our destination.

The Odyssey of Clyde the Camel

Sally trudged wearily up the stairs and knocked on the door to our room.

"What took you so long, Grandma? It's almost dark," Julie asked.

"I was having such fun I lost track of the time. God, do my feet hurt!"

The next morning Sally's feet were still aching, but she wasn't going to let that stop her.

"I'm going to have to wear some different shoes. These made blisters on my feet."

She brought out a pair of sandals and put them on.

"Ahh. That feels better than the tennis shoes."

After checking her map to see where to head that day, Sally led us out of the hotel room. We went downstairs and into the street.

"What about breakfast?" Jason inquired.

"Yeah, I'm hungry," Julie added.

"You guys never eat breakfast," Sally commented.

"That's 'cause we sleep late," Jason replied.

"Okay, we'll grab some pastries at the patisserie and take them with us."

"I want one of those breads with the chocolate in the middle," Jason said

We stopped and got the pastries and were soon on our way.

"Where are we going today, Grandma?" Julie inquired.

"*Montmartre,* to see the *Moulin Rouge* and *Sacré Coeur.*"

"What are those?" Jason asked.

"Montmartre is where a lot of famous artists lived and worked. The Moulin Rouge means Red Mill. That's where the Can-Can dancers perform and Sacré Coeur is a well-known beautiful church."

"Sounds boring to me," Jason remarked.

"Too bad. I'm in charge. You might actually enjoy it."

We took the now-familiar walk to the Metro and got on board the fast-moving subway car.

When we got off at our stop, Jason asked, "Is that the Moulin Rouge?" pointing to a building with a large windmill on top of it.

"Yep, that's it."

"It looks pretty cool."

They quickly walked over to the famous landmark and Sally immediately took out her camera and started taking pictures.

"This might be a good time to eat an early lunch," Sally said. "I know you guys are always ready to eat."

We walked across the street to a sidewalk café and sat down. A young man wearing a starched white shirt, black pants and an apron approached carrying three menus.

"Bon Jour. Bienvenu au Café Gaugin (*Good day. Welcome to Café Gaugin*)."

"Merci," Sally replied.

"May I get you some beverages, Madame? My name is Henri and I am at your service," the waiter replied, suddenly breaking into perfect English.

"Well, I guess your French isn't that good," Jason

joked.

Sally's face turned red.

"Yes, please. I'll have water and I guess my two grandchildren will have soda, right?" she asked looking at Jason and Julie.

"I'll take a Coke," Jason said.

"Me, too," Julie added.

"Very good, I'll get your drinks right away. And, Madame I'm sure you speak French very well, no matter what your children say."

"Thank you, but they're not my children. They're my grandchildren," Sally responded.

"Oh, no. Not possible, Madame. You are too young to have grandchildren," the waiter said.

This time Sally's face turned the same shade as the red in the plaid fur of my Scottish Terrier chum, Fergus MacPherson.

Henri soon returned with the drinks. In the meantime, Sally had taken me out of her tote bag and had placed me on the chair next to her, much to Jason and Julie's embarrassment.

"I see you have one more joining you for lunch, your petit chameau (*little camel*)."

"His name is Clyde. We got him in England."

"Have you decided what you want to eat?" Henri inquired.

"I'll have the omelet, my granddaughter will have the chicken sandwich and he'll have the hamburger with pommes frites (French fries)," pointing to Jason.

When the food arrived, Sally and the kids ate eagerly.

I guess all the walking had given them an appetite.

Am I ever going to get to eat crepes? I thought.

Sally paid Henri, said "Bonne journee" *(Have a good day)* and we were on our way.

Our next stop was Sacré Coeur, a very famous church. It was started in 1875 and took sixteen years to finish.

The humans had to walk up what seemed like a gazillion steps. They were almost all the way to the top of the hill when the kids told Sally she could go the rest of the way without them because they didn't want to see "some old church."

"Suit yourselves. Wait right here and DON'T MOVE."

"Yeah, Yeah. We know the drill, Grandma," Jason replied.

When Sally got to the top she looked with dismay at the throngs of people gathered outside the basilica.

"It will take me forever to get inside," she said. "I think I'll just take some pictures and look at the beautiful views of the city."

From the top you could see almost all of Paris. The Eiffel Tower stood out in the distance and you could see the Arc de Triomphe.

Sally went back to meet Jason and Julie. To her pleasant surprise they were right where she had left them.

"Hey, guys. There's a cable car that we can ride down to the bottom to save walking. It's just a few steps up."

"That sounds great," Julie remarked.

The Odyssey of Clyde the Camel

After the descent Jason inquired, "Where are we going next, Grandma?"

"I thought we'd see *Père Lachaise Cemetery*. Jim Morrison is buried there."

"A cemetery! And who the heck is Jim Morrison?" Jason exclaimed.

"He was a famous rock and roll star," Julie explained, beaming with pride that she knew something Jason didn't know. "Grandma Rogers told me all about him. She asked me to take pictures of his grave."

"Well, count me out," Jason said.

"I'll tell you what, Jason. We'll go back to the hotel, leave you there and Julie and I will go by ourselves."

"Sounds good to me."

We hopped on the Metro and were soon back at the hotel.

It was just a short ride to the famous cemetery where many well-known people are buried. I found out that singers, politicians and writers had their final resting place here. There were graves of many ordinary people here also.

"Julie, did you know that anyone can be buried here? You just have to pay for the plot, but guess what happens if your family don't keep up the payments? They move your body."

"That sounds gross," Julie observed.

We found Jim Morrison's final resting place with just a plain gravestone to mark the plot. A crowd was peering at the hallowed ground and speaking in hushed tones. Fans, probably, had placed fresh flowers on the marker and around the grave.

Jim Morrison's grave at Père Lachaise Cemetery

"You know. I think this is where I want to be buried when my time comes. I'll just have someone come and sprinkle my ashes here. Then it won't cost anything," Sally said, half in jest.

"That's really morbid to think about, Grandma."

"Well, we'd better head back to the hotel. Jason's probably hungry by now.

Chapter 6
Meeting New Friends

The next morning it was time to say "Au Revoir" to Paris. Sally had made arrangements for a taxi to pick us up and take us to the train station for the next leg of our trip.

Promptly at 8:00 a.m., the cab arrived.

"Mon Dieu (*My God*). You have a lot of bags. It will cost extra for this, Madame," the driver said.

"Yes, I know," Sally said, sighing.

After a ten-minute ride we were at the *Gare de Lyon*. The driver unloaded the bags, Sally handed him the fare and we made our way to the ticket counter. Sally spoke to the ticket agent in French, told her our destination was *Montbeliard* and purchased the tickets. I must say, she was getting to be a pro at this.

Jason and Julie were soon in dreamland, while Sally and I enjoyed the scenery. The two-hour ride went by fast and before we knew it we were pulling into the station.

"Wake up Julie. Wake up Jason. We're here."

Everyone gathered their belongings and stepped off the train.

"There's Louis," Sally said pointing to a smiling grey-haired man.

She waved and beckoned the kids to follow her.

"Sally, Sally. So good to see you," Louis said.

I could tell that he had been practicing those words in English. He had a friendly voice and a nice smile.

"Oh, Louis. It's been too long. We are so happy to be here."

Jason and Julie were hanging back.

"Louis, voici mes petits-enfants (*These are my grandchildren*), Jason and Julie."

"Very pleased to meet you," he said, holding out his hand.

The two stepped forward and shook his hand.

Louis gasped as he looked at all the luggage and then looked at the small Peugeot he was driving. It was amazing that everything fit in the car.

After a short ride to nearby *Exincourt*, where Sally's friends lived, we arrived at Louis' home and were greeted by Jeanne, his wife.

She kissed Sally back and forth on both cheeks twice and started helping us inside with the luggage.

"Jasoon and Julee you sleep là-bas," Jeanne said, pointing to a cosy-looking room.

"Oh, good. I get to have my own room," Sally said, just loud enough for me to hear.

"Sally, you sleep là-bas," pointing to the basement stairs. "Is okay?"

The Odyssey of Clyde the Camel

"C'est parfait (*It's perfect*)."

She maneuvered carefully down the narrow steps with one suitcase and tote bag while Louis followed behind carrying the other suitcase.

"This *is* perfect," Sally said to me as she started unpacking. "My own bathroom and everything. No more picking up Julie and Jason's wet towels from the floor. Plenty of hot water and no more checking to make sure the shower control isn't set at "scalding" before I get in."

Before long, delicious aromas were coming from the kitchen and we headed upstairs to see what was cooking.

"Le sous-sol (*basement*) is okay, Sally?" Jeanne inquired.

"Magnifique" (*magnificent*)!" Sally responded. "Ou est Jason et Julie?" (*Where are Jason and Julie*)?"

Jeanne held out her hands in front of her, palms open and touching, with her head facing down pantomiming someone looking at a phone. They both laughed.

"Qui est votre petit ami? (*Who is your little friend*)?" Jeanne asked, pointing at me.

"Il est Clyde. (*He's Clyde*)."

Très mignon. (*Very cute*)."

I could feel my face turning red. I think that's called blushing.

After dinner. Sally said good night to everyone.

"Don't stay up too late, guys. We've got a lot to do tomorrow."

We headed downstairs to our cosy pad and were soon fast asleep.

"I can't believe I slept so late," Sally said the next

morning looking at the clock on the wall. "It's almost eight o'clock."

We went upstairs to find Jeanne and Louis in the kitchen drinking coffee and reading the newspaper.

"Est-ce que tu as bien dormi? (*Did you sleep well*)?" Jacqueline inquired.

"Comme une bûche (*Like a log*)," Sally answered.

When ten o'clock rolled around, it took a combined effort of Sally, Jeanne and Louis to rouse Jason and Julie from their deep sleep. They used all the techniques known to man – tickling, prodding, threatening and finally yelling "your bed's on fire!" to get them to wake up.

Julie sleepily opened her eyes and gave Sally a dirty look.

"Leave us alone, Grandma. We're on vacation," she howled.

"Vacation doesn't mean sleeping all day. It means having fun. We're going to the *Peugeot Museum*."

"Another museum!" Jason whined, now fully awake.

"Yes, but not a boring one. This one has lots of cars in it. We might even get to visit the Peugeot factory where Louis used to work."

"Oh, great. Just what I want to see – a bunch of cars and people working," Julie sneered.

"No griping allowed. Remember the rules. No griping, no fighting and no disrespectful attitude. You've already broken all of them. You're not going to embarrass me in front of my friends."

"Okay. We'll be ready in a few minutes."

"Thirty minutes. That's all," Sally retorted. "You can have some toast made with delicious French bread and some coffee, if you want. You need something to get you going."

The Peugeot Museum in Sochaux, France

At 10:30 on the dot, Jeanne, the rest of the group, and I left for the museum in nearby *Sochaux*.

It was brilliant! There were all kinds of old and new cars – from race cars to family sedans. They even had something called concept cars. We saw old bicycles, motorbikes, tools, sewing machines, coffee grinders and other neat stuff that the company used to manufacture. Jason and Julie had fun sitting in some of the cars and pretending they were racing down the road at 150 kilometers per hour.

We didn't get to see the factory because by the time we left the museum we had to go back to the house for lunch.

"Louis aura faim (*Louis will be hungry*)," Jeanne explained.

Arriving back at home, Jeanne put the finishing touches on the meal she had started to prepare that morning.

We feasted on coq au vin and fresh vegetables. It looked delicious. Too bad I didn't get to eat anything. The meal ended with a plate of assorted cheeses and for dessert, a scrumptious-looking peach pie. Sally kept remarking how delicious everything tasted and what a good cook Jeanne was. Even the usually picky eaters asked for seconds.

After the meal, Sally helped Jeanne clean up the kitchen and Louis took the kids down to the basement to look at his radio-controlled aeroplanes.

When the dishes were done, we took a walk with Jeanne while Louis retired to the salon to watch telly. Jason and Julie went to their room to catch up with their Facebook friends and post pictures.

The next few days passed quickly and, before we knew, it was time to get packed again and prepare for the next part of our journey. I had come to have warm feelings for these nice people, but I was excited about embarking on the rest of my "odyssey" as Sally was beginning to call our trip.

Chapter 7
Misadventures

The day started like many other days on our journey. By the time it was over, though, it would become "the day from hell," as Sally put it.

We all woke up early because we had to catch the train to *Toulouse*. After the packing was finished, we said our goodbyes to Jeanne and Louis. Sally held back tears as she hugged Jeanne good-by. She looked very sad. Sally told me later it was because she was afraid that it would be a long time before she would see them again.

The four of us, along with all our luggage, again piled into Louis' minuscule Peugeot. Again I was amazed that everything fit. It reminded me of the circus clowns all piled into a teeny-tiny car on a programme I'd seen on the telly. He drove us back to the train station we had arrived at, said "Bientot" (*See you later*) and "Bonne Chance!" (*Good luck*) as we boarded the train.

The ride was a lot of fun and we saw some

interesting scenery. In *Montpellier* we had to change trains. The station was very large and it took us a long time to find the right track. By the time we got there, the train was there and ready to leave. The humans had a hard time getting all their bags on board and locating a place to sit.

Sally couldn't find a place at her seat for her large suitcase, so she had to leave it in one of the breezeways between the cars.

"I don't think it will be a problem. I did it before on my last trip to France and nothing happened," she said to me.

Sally settled down in her seat and picked up her book to read. Julie and Jason were already asleep with their heads on the fold-down trays.

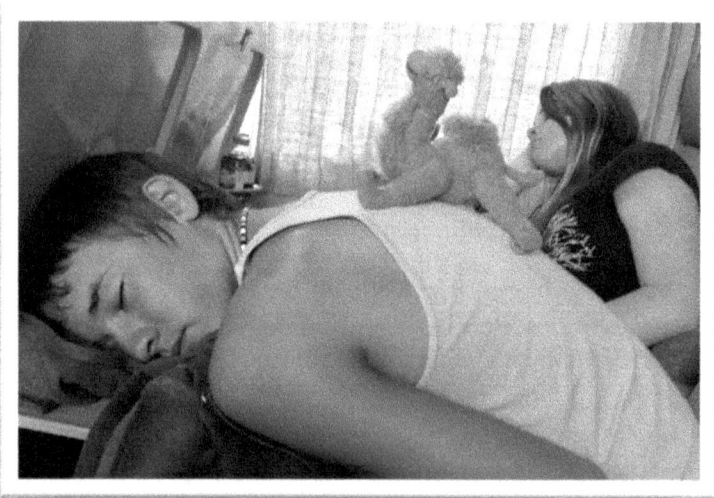

Jason & Julie asleep on the train

The Odyssey of Clyde the Camel

The train stopped at many quaint villages and each time people got off and got on. Finally, when we were almost to Toulouse, Sally went to get her suitcase. It wasn't there!

She searched every car, looking at the overhead bins and between the seats, but it was nowhere to be found. Dismayed, she returned to her seat.

"My suitcase is gone!" Sally announced to the kids.

"Oh, no, Grandma," Jason said. "What are you going to do?"

"Well, I'll have to report it to the railroad people when we get to Toulouse."

As the train pulled into the station, Sally looked at me and sighed. "I don't think I'm ever going to see my suitcase again."

They disembarked and Sally immediately told a man in a uniform about her missing bag.

"You must go to Baggage Perdu *(Lost Luggage)*," he replied.

"Where is that?" Sally inquired.

He gave her directions and she set out with Julie and Jason trailing behind. Sally learned that she had to go to another office in a different part of the building and fill out a form.

"You stay here with all the luggage," she said to the pair. "Keep an eye on everything."

Sally went to the designated place and found that it was closed.

"Just my luck."

She headed back to where Jason and Julie were supposed to be waiting. They were gone!

"Oh, great!" she exclaimed.

Actually she said something else, but I'm not supposed to use those kinds of words.

Just then she saw Julie waving to her.

"Why did you guys move when I told you to stay right where I left you?"

"We couldn't get a good Wi-Fi signal," Julie replied.

"Okay. Well, let's go pick up our car."

We made our way to the car rental office at the train station and Sally got the car keys. They found the automobile and loaded all the suitcases and gear into the trunk.

"Grandma, are you sure you know how to drive a stick shift?" Jason asked.

"Well, it's been a while, but I think I'll do okay."

Vroom. The engine started up. Sally put the car in reverse and slowly backed out of the parking space.

"Grandma, be careful," Julie interjected.

The car promptly stalled. Jason and Julie started snickering.

"Maybe you should have gotten an automatic," Jason remarked.

"No back seat driving, guys."

Sally shifted into first gear and we got out of the parking lot.

"Okay, Jason. Look at the map and tell me what street we need to turn on."

"Doesn't the car have a GPS?"

"We don't need a GPS. We have a map."

Sally glanced at the map and found the street where the hotel was located.

Toulouse train station

"It looks like we just have to go down this street two blocks, turn right at the next street and then make another right."

She carefully pulled into the street, shifted into second gear and third gear and drove the two blocks.

"Way to go, Grandma." Jason commented.

At the next street she turned right.

"See, nothing to driving a stick," she remarked.

As they were getting to the street where their hotel was located. Sally saw smoke coming from the front of the car and smelled a really bad smell.

"Something isn't right," she said.

"Yeah, THE CAR'S ON FIRE!" Julie screamed.

"It's not on fire. It's just overheating. I'd better pull over."

Amazingly enough, she found a parking spot, pulled in, raised the hood and took a look.

Immediately, two men came over.

"Très mauvais. (*Very bad*)," one observed.

"L'automobile ne marche pas. (*The car doesn't run*)," Sally said.

The other man stuck his head under the hood and started fiddling with some wires.

Sally looked at the number on the building they were parked next to, then glanced down at the paper with her hotel reservations written on it.

"Guys, we're just down the street from the hotel. I'm going to walk down, use their phone and call the car rental agency. Stay with the car."

Sally thanked the men for their concern and explained in sign language and fractured French that she was going to call for help.

"Listen. Don't leave the car. Keep the doors locked. I'll be back in a few minutes."

She grabbed me from her tote bag and we made our way to the hotel. At the end of the street we both spied the train station. The hotel was only two blocks from where we had started!

After she called the car rental agency and told them the situation, the representative told her they would send a tow truck.

"Don't bother with another car. I just want a complete refund. I only drove it about five blocks."

We then trudged back to the car and Sally told Jason and Julie what was going on.

"We have to stay until the tow truck comes and then we'll get all our stuff and walk to the hotel."

When rescue arrived about a half hour later, Sally and the kids unloaded the car. I was watching everything going on. This wasn't exactly what I had in mind when I said I wanted to have an adventure.

"Wait a second. Where's my laptop? It's not here!" Sally exclaimed.

She checked under and between the seats for the small device. It wasn't in the car.

"You were supposed to be watching the luggage, Julie," Sally cried.

"I did. I took everything when I moved the suitcases."

"Well, apparently, not everything."

"Maybe you left it somewhere else. You know you're always losing things," Jason commented.

"I know I didn't have it with me when I went to report my bag being stolen. The only place it could be is where we were before you moved everything. Or maybe I left it at the car rental office."

"Ah, you'll find it Grandma. Remember when you thought you had lost the walkie-talkies and then they showed up."

"Yes, I remember how they mysteriously re-appeared after I practically tore the hotel room in London all apart," Sally responded, sarcastically.

They slogged wearily to the hotel, checked in and carried the bags up to their rooms.

"I'm going back to the train station and see if there's any chance it's still there. I'll be back in a little while. Then we can go have something to eat."

Sally and I returned to the train station and she described the missing laptop to the young lady working at the lunch counter, hoping someone might have found it and turned it in.

"Non, Madame. Votre ordinateur n'est pas ici (*No, Madam. Your computer is not here*)."

"D'Accord. Merci. (*Okay. Thank you*). "I'd better order something for the kids while I'm here," she said to me. "I know they'll be hungry."

While the young lady was making the sandwiches, Sally re-traced their steps from where they had been sitting to where the kids had moved all the luggage. She looked under the table. No computer.

She went back to the lunch counter, picked up the sandwiches and trekked back to the hotel.

"Did you find it, Grandma?" Julie asked.

"What do you think?" Sally responded. "Are you sure you're not hiding it from me as a joke? Because if you are, now would be a good time to 'fess up."

"We promise we aren't, Grandma," Jason replied.

"Okay. Well, goodnight. I'm exhausted and I'm going to bed. Here are some sandwiches for you."

"Thanks, Grandma. Aren't you going to eat?" Jason asked.

"I'm not hungry."

"Goodnight, Grandma. I love you and sorry about the computer," Julie said quietly.

"I love you guys, too. Don't stay up too late. I'm going back to the car rental agency first thing in the morning and see if I might have left my laptop there. Then I have to go buy some clothes. Most of them were in the missing suitcase. God, what a day!"

Chapter 8
Discovering New Places

Sally woke up the next morning and I could tell by the way she sighed and yawned really wide a few times that she probably hadn't gotten much sleep. She stepped out of bed and tripped over one of the kid's suitcases.

"Crap!!" she yelled. Then glanced over at Julie and Jason. Not a stir.

"The room is on fire!" she shouted.

Julie rolled over in bed. No reaction from either of the "Rip Van Winkles."

"Well, Clyde. At least I have one clean pair of underwear to put on."

She picked up her t-shirt, smelled it, shrugged her shoulders, found her blue jeans next to the bed and finished getting dressed. Then she walked downstairs for breakfast. After eating, Sally went back to the room.

"Well, Clyde, I see that Tweedledee and

Tweedledum are still sleeping."

She walked over to their beds and started shaking them.

"Wake up, you guys. I'm going out for a walk. Stay here in the room until I get back or if you want to go down and have something to eat, I'll leave some money for you."

"Okay, okay. We're up," Jason replied testily.

"I'll be back in an hour or so. Then maybe you guys will be ready to do a little sightseeing."

Sally walked hurriedly back to the train station and entered the car rental office.

"And how are you doing, today, Madame? How can I help you?" the young man said, smiling his perfect customer service smile.

"Not that great. You remember me from yesterday. I rented the car from you. I guess you heard about the problem."

"Oh, yes. And I am so sorry. I can arrange for another car, if you like."

"That won't be necessary. I just want to make sure I will get a full refund. Oh, and I came to see if I might have left a small laptop computer here."

"We did not find a computer, Madame, but you are free to look around." Sally scoured the small office, but found nothing.

She said good-bye to the man and walked out of the office. Then she proceeded to the Baggage Perdu office, filled out the form and walked towards the hotel. Glancing at her watch, she saw that only twenty minutes had passed.

"Julie and Jason are probably just now rolling out of bed, Clyde. I'm going to look for a store where I can buy some cheap clothes."

Sally walked a few blocks, spotted a small boutique and walked in. A big grin came over her face.

"My kind of place. A thrift shop."

She entered the small store and looked around. After she gathered a few articles of clothing, she asked the clerk where the dressing rooms were.

Sally found a couple of tops, a skirt and a pair of jeans that fit and took them to the counter. Then remembering something else, she picked out some underwear and a bra and placed them with the rest of the clothes.

"Twelve euros, Madame," the clerk said.

Sally handed her the money and said "Merci."

"Bonne journée, Madame (*Have a good day, Madame*)," the young lady replied.

"Oui, bonne journée," Sally answered.

She quickly walked back to the hotel. She looked happy that she had accomplished her mission and seemed in a much better mood.

To her surprise, Julie and Jason were dressed.

"Did you find your laptop?" Julie asked.

Sally shook her head.

"Have you guys eaten?"

"Yeah, we went downstairs and had chocolate milk and pastries," Jason answered.

"Do you feel like going out and seeing some sights?"

Sally inquired. "There's a neat sounding museum of natural history here. The guidebook says they have fossils, dinosaur bones and other cool stuff."

"Yeah, that sounds pretty good," Julie said.

"Well, let's get going then."

We went downstairs and Sally asked the man at reception the best way to get to the *Toulouse Museum.* He showed her on the map, told her what Metro stop to walk to, which way to go on the Metro and where to get off.

Clyde at the Toulouse Museum

The museum was brilliant with all kinds of neat exhibits. There was a real stuffed elephant. Just wait 'til I tell Ellen, my elephant friend back in Marazion. Gosh, I hadn't even thought of my chums for a long time. I hope they're doing okay and haven't forgotten about me.

We saw a demonstration of how an earthquake feels. It was so real I got kind of scared. There were ecological exhibits and, of course, lots of fossils.

After we finished going through the museum it was time for (what else?) lunch.

Later, Sally and I went back to the train station. She told me later she could have done it blindfolded by then. Uhmm. I'd like to see that. She needed to buy train tickets for the following day. We were going to another town in the area called *Pau*. That's where some other friends of hers lived.

So, bright and early the next day we were back on another train. I've decided that's the best way to travel. You get to places real fast and see lots of neat scenery and you don't have to fight traffic or worry about cars breaking down.

This time Sally only had to worry about one suitcase and her tote bag. She couldn't help chuckling at Julie and Jason as they struggled with their bags.

As our train pulled into the station at Pau I saw a smiling woman with short hair standing on the platform. She looked familiar, even though I knew I had never seen her before. Sally went to the window and waved.

"It's Marie, Jeanne and Louis' daughter!"

Now I knew why she looked familiar. She had the same smiling, happy look on her face as her mother.

Sally, Julie and Jason gathered their belongings and stepped off the train. Marie wrapped her arms around Sally and gave her a big hug, then went over to Julie and Jason and hugged them.

The Odyssey of Clyde the Camel

She helped the gang put the suitcases into her car, started the engine and pulled out of the parking lot.

"It's not very far to your hotel. We be there in ten minutes."

Marie spoke English pretty well. Sally made sure that she didn't speak too fast so that Marie could understand and threw in a little French here and there.

When we pulled up to the *Èco Relais Hotel* everyone grabbed a suitcase or back pack and carried them into the lobby.

"I'll wait for you downstairs and then we go back to my apartment for dinner," Marie said.

"Très bon. J'ai faim (*Very good. I'm hungry*)," replied Sally. "And I'm sure the kids are, too."

Soon we were back in the car and making our way to another part of town. Marie was showing the gang some of the sights with one hand on the steering wheel and one pointing out the window gesturing; one eye on the road and one looking at the buildings; passing cars; honking and saying some words in French I didn't understand. One sounded like "mare." Sally told me about this later; I was safely tucked away in her tote bag.

At Marie's apartment, we met Pierre and Claudine, her nine-year-old twins. They immediately made friends with me and I decided French children are really nice.

After dinner we watched a football match on T.V. Not the American kind - the European kind that you Americans call soccer. Pierre was yelling and clapping for his favorite team. Claudine was sitting at the table coloring. Marie and Sally were in the kitchen doing the dishes and Jason and Julie were on the couch on their mobiles. Sally told Marie about the mishap with the suitcase and laptop.

"Mon Dieu (*My God*)!" Marie exclaimed. "Merdre!"

There was that word again.

"J'ai acheté des vêtements dans un magasin à Toulouse. (I *bought some clothes at a shop in Toulouse*)"

"I might have some clothes to fit you," Marie said.

She brought out a pair of jeans and a t-shirt. Sally thanked her and went in the bedroom to try them on.

"Parfait (*Perfect*)," she said, as she came back into the living room. "Now my wardrobe is complete."

Later that evening, Marie took us back to the hotel and we climbed into bed. Even Jason and Julie were soon fast asleep.

Clyde at the aquarium

The Odyssey of Clyde the Camel

The following day, Marie was there to take us on a sightseeing tour of the town. She showed us a brochure with a picture of fish on it.

"Would the children like to see an aquarium?" Marie asked.

"That sounds like a great idea. How about it, guys?" Sally replied.

"Yeah. I think that would be fun," Julie said.

So we all piled into Marie's car and she drove us to the *Aquarium Tropical des Pyrénées*. They had all kinds of live fish there. The only fish I've ever seen was Dory, my friend at The New Curiosity Shop.

The next day was Jason's birthday, so Sally and Marie had the idea to surprise him with a cake. They went to the local "supermarché" (*supermarket*), bought a birthday cake, candles and a pizza for dinner.

Everyone eagerly anticipated the cake after they had their fill of pizza. Marie brought it out and set it on the table. Sally placed the candles in the cake and lit them.

"Now make a wish and blow out the candles, Jason," Sally said.

He took a deep breath and blew out the candles which instantly came back to life. Pierre and Claudine giggled as Jason tried repeatedly to blow out the candles. Everyone agreed that the cake was delicious. It sure looked delicious. Too bad I couldn't have any.

"Well, we'd better be getting back to the hotel," Sally said finally. "Janet is coming in the morning to take us on another day trip."

Janet was Sally's friend that she had known for many

years. She lived in the nearby town of *Ger*. They had not seen each other for a long time and Sally was excited about reconnecting.

Janet showed up at the Eco Relais promptly at 10:00. The kids were dressed and eager to go to the *Grottes de Bétharram*.

"Sally, it's great to see you!" Janet exclaimed.

Janet had an accent that I hadn't heard in a long time. Blimey she was a limey! Okay, so I'm a very bad poet.

I found out that Janet was from England but had lived in France for over twenty years. She spoke fluent French and taught English to business people.

"You look fantastic, Janet! This is Jason and Julie."

"Nice to meet you. Sally has told me so much about you."

The two women exchanged knowing glances.

We hopped into Janet's car and were soon making our way out of town.

"I think you'll really enjoy this place, guys," Janet said, looking in the rear view mirror at Julie and Jason.

We soon arrived at the Grottes. We went inside a building and Janet bought the tickets.

The Grottes de Bétharram were awesome! I've decided not to use "brilliant" too much.

They are a series of underground caves that you can walk through. We even rode in a little boat on a subterranean river. The stalactites and stalagmites were super. It was so cold down there that everyone buttoned up their jackets. Of course, my fur kept me plenty warm.

After the cave tour we had lunch and then Janet

drove us back to her house. She lived in a two-story cottage on about an acre. The kids enjoyed playing with the cat, dog and chickens that were running around the yard. Actually, the mean-looking rooster kind of scared me. Soon it was time to go back to the hotel.

"I wish we could have longer to visit," Sally remarked.

"Me, too," replied Janet.

"You have to come back to Florida sometime soon. Remember how much you enjoyed the beach and Disney World when you were there before."

"I love Florida. I might just do that."

Janet and Sally hugged each other, promising to keep in touch. Then Janet gave Julie and Jason a big hug.

"It was nice meeting you."

"Yeah. We had a good time. Thanks for taking us to the caves," Julie replied.

"You'll have to tell me all about the rest of your trip on Facebook. I'll friend you."

Chapter 9
Andorra & the Cirque du Soleil

The next country we were to visit was one that Sally had never been to before. She told me later that it was one of the most interesting places she had ever seen. *Andorra* is a small country between France and Spain. It's high up in the *Pyrénées Mountains*. The people in Andorra speak *Catalan*, a language that is similar to Spanish but very different also.

The only way you could get into the country at that time was by car, bus, bicycle, motorbike or by hiking. Sally decided the best way to go was by bus since she hadn't ridden a bicycle in a while and her recent experience with renting a car had not gone very well. Motor bike was definitely out of the question and hiking would have been impossible with all their luggage. I could have made it, though. Camels can walk a long way.

As soon as we stepped off the bus, I felt like I had been transported to a fairy tale kingdom. Now, you are probably wondering how a stuffed camel who has never been to school knows about fairy tales. Well, Ian, (you know, the cheeky lad I used to live with). His mum read him fairy tales when he was little. The book she read from had fantastic colour pictures in it. Andorra looked just like those pictures.

Hotel Santa Barbara de la Vall d'Ordino

The bus dropped us off just two blocks from *Hotel Santa Barbara de la Vall d'Ordino*. It was made from large stones. In fact, all the buildings in the village of *Ordino* were built from the same material.

There was a sign in English and several other languages on the hotel's front door, saying "Reception is closed. Come back at 3:00."

Sally and the kids didn't seem to care, even though

they had had a long day.

"Guess what time it is?" Sally asked.

"Time to eat!" Jason exclaimed.

"You're right, kiddo."

After everyone ate, we went to check in. The nice lady at reception gave Sally two room keys and the troop made their way upstairs. The room was actually a two-level suite with two bathrooms. Jason and Julie staked their claim to the upper level and Sally settled into the lower suite.

"Wow, no having to listen to Grandma snore for the next couple of nights," Jason rejoiced.

"Yes! Privacy and my own bathroom!" Sally exclaimed. "Clyde and I are going to be really comfortable here."

My very own bed! I thought.

When Sally went down to explore, she stopped to talk with Maria, the front desk clerk. She noticed a sign advertising *Cirque du Soleil*. There was going to be a free performance in the nearby town of *Andorra la Vella* the next evening.

"How do I get tickets?" she asked Maria.

"Just go on the internet and order them. We have free WiFi here, you know."

"Yes. My grandchildren have already discovered that."

Sally logged on with her smart phone and reserved three tickets to be picked up at the gate.

"Clyde, we're going to Cirque du Soleil tomorrow. This should impress Julie and Jason," she told me as we walked back up the stairs.

I knew that "cirque" meant "circus" in French. My friend Alphonse, the stuffed French Poodle, had been teaching me the language.

"Eet eese very important to improve ourselves. Learning a new language eese one of zee best ways and of course French is zee best language to learn," he had told me once.

I only hoped that this was going to be a real circus with real live animals and not a fake one like Piccadilly Circus in London.

The following afternoon, we all got on a local bus for the twenty minute ride to Andorra la Vella. Sally had told the kids we were going early so we could be sure and get a good spot to sit. There would probably be a large crowd at the performance and it would be "first come, first served."

The town was larger than the small village of Ordino with a lot of modern buildings and traffic. Not as big as London or Paris, though.

Sally glanced at her map and followed it as they walked along the river. Soon they were at the Parc Central. Sally went to the gate, gave the attendant her name and picked up the free tickets. They found a good spot close to the stage.

"You hold our places," Sally said to the kids, "while I go find something to eat. And..."

"I know. Don't move," Julie interjected.

"I want a hamburger," Jason said.

"I'll have a chicken sandwich," said Julie.

Shortly, Sally returned with the food. They ate and watched the park start to fill up with people of all ages.

Around 7:30 there was a buzz of excitement. Some of the performers were mingling with the crowd, doing tricks and posing for pictures.

Bring on the animals, I thought to myself.

Clyde & Sally at the Cirque du Soleil

But no animals showed up. I guess I'll have to wait to see a real circus some other time.

The performance was brilliant, though. Acrobatics, trapeze artists, music, everything. The costumes were so colourful! Everyone enjoyed the show, including me.

The next day, Sally and the kids did some hiking up a hill next to the hotel. Then Julie and Jason went back to their room to post pictures on Facebook.

Sally knew by now there was no point in getting them interested in sightseeing, so she visited a small country church. She walked around admiring the architecture and the interesting modern sculptures in the town square.

"You know, Clyde, I could live here. It's so quiet and peaceful and the people are so friendly."

Chapter 10
Olé for Barcelona

Too soon it was time to leave this beautiful idyllic country and depart for the last leg of our odyssey - Spain. Sally was up early, as usual. She finished her packing, then decided to go down for breakfast. She went to the kids' room to wake them.

"You'd better get something to eat. It's going to be a long trip and I'm out of food bars. If you don't eat here at the hotel, you're going to have to pay for a snack out of your spending money."

"Okay, Grandma," Jason replied sleepily.

They walked to the nearby bus stop to catch the local bus for Andorra la Vella where they would catch another bus to Barcelona.

Almost as soon as the four of us were on the second bus, Jason and Julie were fast asleep in the back. Sally sat up front where she could get a good view. After a journey of a couple of hours through scenic mountains,

The Odyssey of Clyde the Camel

we crossed the border into Spain and were soon in Barcelona. Olé! That's Spanish for "Hurray." They shout it at bullfights which really aren't two bulls fighting each other. It's a bunch of men ganging up on one bull, torturing it with spears and little darts until the matador finally kills the bull with a sword. People seem to enjoy the spectacle, but I don't think the bull has much fun. I was sure hoping that we weren't going to go to a bull fight.

The *Del Mar Hotel* was right in the middle of downtown Barcelona but on a quiet street surrounded by old buildings. For the very last time on our trip we checked in, got our room keys and unpacked.

"I see from the map, that we're pretty close to the beach," Sally told the kids. "Do you wanna take a walk down there?"

"Sure, let's go," Jason said eagerly.

"You don't want to eat first?"

"Nah. I'm not hungry."

Well, there's a first time for everything, I thought.

A cool breeze was blowing, as we walked along the avenue. People were passing by, some hurriedly, some strolling leisurely. Men and women were sipping wine in the sidewalk cafés. A boy whizzed by on a skateboard. A lady was pushing a pram.

The sun was still shining brightly, even though it was almost 7:00, when we got to the beach. Julie and Jason put their towels in the sand, took their shoes off and ran towards the water.

"I'll watch the stuff. You guys go have fun," Sally

called out to them.

"This is heaven," Sally said dreamily as she stretched out on the towel and closed her eyes.

Clyde at Barcelona Beach

The next day the two of us were up early, as usual, and the kids were "nestled all snug in their beds" while visions of Facebook danced in their heads. Sally wanted to go downstairs for the breakfast buffet and get fueled up for a busy day of sightseeing.

The Odyssey of Clyde the Camel

When we returned to the room, Jason and Julie were still sleeping.

"Okay, Clyde. This is ridiculous. Let's wake them up."

Sally proceeded to tickle Jason.

"Quit it, Grandma," he protested.

Then she went over to Julie and did the same thing.

"Leave me alone, Grandma. I wanna sleep some more."

"Here's the deal. These are the last three days of our vacation. How about we do a little sightseeing this morning and then this afternoon we'll go to the beach?"

"That sounds like a good idea," said Jason, his face brightening up at the word "beach."

"Will an hour give you enough time?"

"Yeah," replied Julie.

While the kids were getting ready, Sally looked through the guidebook to find something that might interest them.

"This sounds cool, guys. There's a big aquarium and an IMAX right near the beach. We could go there and then go swimming."

"Okay," replied Jason.

The kids were ready to go in record time and soon the four of us were walking down the broad avenue. On our way to the waterfront, it was Jason who stopped to take pictures. He noticed boys about his age riding bikes over makeshift ramps.

"Gee. I wish I had my bike here or at least my skateboard. These are some cool places to ride."

This time it was Julie and Sally who rolled their eyes and laughed.

Suddenly, Sally spotted something that looked familiar. There in the square was a statue of Christopher Columbus. She dug into her tote bag until she came across a black and white photo. It was a picture of a girl a little younger than Julie and a lady.

"Guys, this is me and my mom taken when we visited here a long time ago. This is the same statue! Walk on over there. I want to get a picture of you two in front of Christopher Columbus."

For once, Jason and Julie didn't grumble about having their picture taken. In fact, they enjoyed hamming it up. Jason even offered to take a picture of Sally in front of the famous explorer's statue.

We continued walking towards *L'Aquarium Barcelona*. When we got there Sally bought the tickets for the attraction and the IMAX movie. The kids enjoyed looking at all the live sea creatures and the movie was so real I felt like I was actually underwater. I wasn't even scared.

"This is a cool place, Grandma," Jason observed. "Thanks for bringing us here."

"And the IMAX was awesome," Julie added. "Better than the one back home."

True to Sally's word, we walked over to the beach and the kids staked out a place for their towels.

"I'll tell you what. I'm going to leave you guys here for a few hours and go do some more sightseeing. You've got some spending money when you get hungry. You should know your way back to the hotel by now and I've written the name and address on this piece of paper, just in case. Just be sure you're back by 5:00. And put on sunscreen, for heaven's sake. I don't want you to look like lobsters when I take you home."

"Okay, Grandma," Jason replied. "And *we* won't get lost."

"Remember. 5:00 and not a minute later."

Sally, walked away, glancing back at the kids who were already racing towards the surf.

"I hope I'm not making a mistake, Clyde. If anyone kidnaps them, they'll probably pay me to take them back."

Sally consulted her map and we made our way to the center of town.

"Next stop the *Sagrada Familia*, Clyde."

Here was another new language. And I was just starting to understand French.

"That's the Church of the Holy Family, one of the most famous churches in the world according to my guidebook."

We caught the Metro and as soon as we got to our stop, we ascended the stairs to street level. Right before our eyes were the towering spires of this beautiful landmark. They reminded me of something out of a science fiction film I had seen. You've probably guessed by now, I'm a cinema "junkie."

We also saw the long queue that seemed to go on forever and we got behind about a thousand other people.

"It looks like we're going to be here forever," Sally said.

A man in front of her turned around to see who she was speaking to.

"This is just the queue to buy tickets. We'll probably have to come back later to get inside," the man said in a very British accent.

Sally settled in for a long wait and read some information from her guidebook. The Sagrada Familia was designed by the architect, Antoni Gaudi and was started in 1882. Over a hundred years later it still isn't finished. Sounds like one of the projects that Ian (the brat) started building with his Legos and never completed.

An hour later, we finally made it to the ticket office.

The Sagrada Familia

"Your ticket is for 3 p.m., Señora," the man behind the counter said, handing Sally her ticket.

She glanced at her watch. It was only noon.

"Gracias, Señor," Sally said, as she placed the ticket

carefully in her wallet.

We walked across the street and entered a sandwich shop. While Sally was waiting to be served, she thumbed through her guidebook.

"There are a lot of places we can explore, Clyde," she said, looking at the colour photographs.

After Sally ate, we walked back to the Metro stop, rode for a while and then hopped off. We were surrounded by interesting-looking buildings. Making sure to mark our spot on her map, Sally proceeded down the avenue. Some of the buildings were old and some looked very modern.

"Hey, Clyde. The guidebook says this one was designed by Gaudi. It sure has the same "outer space" look to it as the church."

After about an hour of walking and taking pictures along the way, Sally headed back the way we had come. We caught the next train in the direction of the Sagrada Familia and were soon back where we had been almost three hours before. The square around the church was still a sea of people.

"Here's the line we need to be in," Sally said, pointing to a sign that said "Ticket Holders Only" in several languages.

It didn't seem much shorter than the one we had been in before, but in just a few minutes we were inside. The afternoon sunlight poured through the elaborate stained-glass windows. People were speaking in hushed tones and admiring the statues. Some were kneeling in the pews and praying.

"This is absolutely amazing, Clyde," Sally whispered.

We spent an hour walking through the Basilica and then Sally said to me, "We'd better be heading back to the hotel."

When we arrived at the Del Mar and made our way up to the room, Jason and Julie were lying on their beds.

"Did you have a good time?" she asked them, observing Julie's bright red face.

"Yeah, it was fun," Jason replied.

"You'd better put some lotion on your face, Julie. Otherwise, you're going to look like a scaly snake by the time we get to Tampa and your mom will kill me for letting you get sun-burned."

"I'm hungry," Jason uttered the familiar phrase.

"Okay, so how about getting changed so we can go have dinner," Sally suggested.

After supper we went back to the hotel. Although it was still daylight, Sally changed into her nightclothes and got ready for bed.

"I'm going to turn in. I have a ten a.m. reservation for a tour at the *Museu Picasso*. You probably don't want to go, do you?" she asked the kids.

"No. We wanna go back to the beach," Jason replied.

"Okay. Make the most of it. Tomorrow is our last day in Barcelona."

When the sun was just coming up, Sally hopped out of bed, dressed and went down for breakfast. Upon returning to the room, she saw the kids still fast asleep.

"Wake up, guys. Have fun today, but you know the

drill. Be careful and meet me back here at 5:00."

"Okay, Grandma," Julie replied sleepily.

We left the hotel and walked to the museum. the tour was in English and the guide explained to our group all about the artwork and about Picasso's life. Pablo Picasso painted a lot of pictures in several different styles. We saw realistic paintings he did in his early years when he was just starting out.

We saw paintings that didn't even look like real people, but they were still pretty ace. I'm sure learning a lot hanging around with Sally. Just wait until I tell all my friends back in Cornwall. Will they be impressed! I wonder if I could learn to paint. I saw a documentary on

Sally at the Picasso Museum

the telly one time about an elephant that painted with his trunk.

That evening after supper, everyone packed their bags to get ready for the next day. It was still daylight when they were finished.

"I'm going to take a walk to the park and get in a little more sightseeing. Do you want to come?" Sally asked Jason and Julie.

"No, that's okay. We'll stay here."

"Suit yourselves. I'll be back before dark."

We strolled to the *Parc de la Ciutadella,* walked through the gates and saw cages. Hey, a zoo! But it was closed. Well, at least I was getting closer to seeing wild animals. Oh, I wish I could have seen a real live camel.

There was a playground where children were swinging happily and riding on the merry-go-round. I was getting dizzy just watching them. We spied a big lake and saw people wading in the water. We also saw some brilliant murals. Maybe someone will paint a mural of me, one day.

Then we heard music coming from another direction. Sally walked towards the sounds. There were people beating on drums and playing guitars. A man was playing the bagpipes. Boy, would my friend, Fergus, be jealous! Sally clapped when the young man playing the strange-looking instrument finished his song.

"Very good," she remarked.

"Gracias, Señorita," he said. "My name is Javi. I am part of a group called *Clancarakol Compañia*. Do you have a special request?"

"Do you know 'Happy Birthday'? Yesterday was my birthday."

"Of course. I will play, 'Happy Birthday' for the nice American lady."

Javi, the park bagpiper

He squeezed the bag, puffed out his cheeks, placed his fingers on the pegs and began playing a rather strange-sounding rendition of the song. It kind of hurt my ears, but Sally seemed to like it and clapped enthusiastically when he was done. Javi bowed low and thanked her again. She said goodbye and we continued on our way through the park. As the sun started to set in the evening sky we walked back to the hotel.

Chapter 11
Home" at Last

The sun shone brightly through our window as the final day of our odyssey dawned. I kind of hated it to end, but I was looking forward to coming to America, seeing M.J., meeting my animal family and living in a real house again.

Sally, Jason and Julie carried their suitcases and back packs downstairs and we checked out of the hotel. Then we walked the four blocks to the bus stop to catch the bus that would take us to Barcelona Airport.

We got there about three hours before the plane was scheduled to depart. Sally told me she didn't want to take any chances on missing the plane.

"You know, Clyde. I'm kind of sad to see this trip end, but I'll be happy to get home."

Me, too, I thought.

Soon, we were boarding the plane and settling in for the long flight to America. My first time on an aeroplane!

The Odyssey of Clyde the Camel

Clyde on the plane to America

At nine p.m. that evening we arrived at Tampa International Airport. We got our luggage from the baggage claim area and were greeted by Sally's husband and the children's parents. Everyone was talking at once and hugging each other.

"So, did you have a good time, guys?" the kids' dad asked.

"Yeah, it was fun. Especially the beach and the aquarium and the IMAX," Jason replied.

"Just think. We went halfway around the world to see things we can see in Florida," Sally whispered to me.

"Did they behave themselves?" the kids' mom asked.

"They were fine," Sally replied, giving me a wink.

"And who's this little guy?" Sally's husband asked, pointing to me.

"That's Clyde, our mascot," said Sally. "And I think he had a good time, too. Didn't you, Clyde?"

Boy, was I tempted to say something!

The next day after sleeping until about noon, Sally rang up M.J.

"How was the trip? You'll have to tell me all about it," said her friend.

"How much time do you have?" Sally joked.

"How's Clyde?"

"Safe and sound. How about coming over later this afternoon?"

Epilogue
How this Story Came to Be

It was so good to see M.J. again. As soon as I was in the car with her, I couldn't contain myself any longer.

"I missed you so much," I cried.

She wasn't freaked out when she heard my first words. In fact, she didn't seem surprised at all.

"Doesn't it seem a little strange that a stuffed animal is talking to you?" I inquired.

"Not at all. I talk to my kids all the time." (That's what she called her cats and dogs). "And they talk back."

"Ohhh," I replied.

I wasn't sure if I should start thinking about finding a new home. I wasn't sure if I wanted to live with a "crazy cat lady."

"My kids are more like people than a lot of so-called 'people' I know," M.J. explained.

I decided right then and there that I was "home" and

I would never be lonely again. Not with so many "brothers" and "sisters" to keep me company.

"This is really amazing, Clyde. Now tell me all about your trip."

After I finished my tale, M.J. decided that people should hear my story. She contacted her writer friend, Sarah.

I must say, Sarah was a little more taken aback by my verbal skills than Mum was, but she soon got used to it. Sarah thought a book about my adventures was a grand idea. And that is how my story came to be.

I hope you liked reading my book and that you'll tell all your friends about it and they'll buy my book and I'll make lots of money. Oh, dear, that sounded a bit brassy, didn't it?

Well, I really would like to be rich. Not for selfish reasons, mind you. I'd give some of the money to my mum and then I would spend some of it to go back to Cornwall and rescue my friends. Then I'd really like to take another trip somewhere. I've heard there are lots of great places to see in America. The Grand Canyon, New York City, Hollywood, Graceland...

Cheers for now!

The Odyssey of Clyde the Camel

The Ballad of Clyde the Camel

Let me tell the tale of a famous camel,
He's my fav'rite dromedary mammal.
Clyde the Camel is his name.
Having fun is his only game.

He likes to travel to far-off places.
All those unfamiliar faces
Gets his engine on the run,
Having lots of camel fun.

Now, Clyde was an orphan a long time ago.
Full of sorrow and of woe.
'Til a girl named M.J. took him on her roam.
And then she finally took him home.

She found Clyde in a second-hand store.
And to him this oath she solemnly swore.
"Oh, Clyde you are the cutest thing.
I want you more than anything."

Clyde was soon on a fabulous trip,
By bus, by train, by ferry ship.
First stop was in London town.
A smile replaced his sad, sad frown.

M.J. was just so much fun.
He knew he'd be the envy of everyone.
Then on to a quiet seaside place.
By train and taxi with much haste.

He swam at the beach, had tea and scones.
It thrilled him down to his camel bones.
Then on to Dover with its cliffs of white.
The ferry would leave by day, not night.

The English Channel they did cross.
The waves his body did hardly toss.
They soon arrived in Calais, France.
Clyde felt like doing a little dance

Then on by train to Gay Paree.
Oh, golly, golly, golly, gee.
The Eiffel Tower was such a sight.
Gustave got it just so right.

The fresh-baked bread smelled so sublime.
He ate it with a glass of wine.
South by train and bus Clyde rode.
For transportation that was his mode.

To tiny Andorra, close to Spain.
The sun was shining, not a drop of rain.
The houses all were made of stone.
The church bell peeled a beautiful tone.

The Odyssey of Clyde the Camel

Clyde's last stop was in nearby Spain.
He felt so proud; he was almost vain.
"If all my friends could see me now,
I know I'd take a graceful bow."

Barcelona was a fabulous town.
The waves on the beach made a lovely sound.
Gaudi's church was a beautiful shrine.
Clyde had never seen anything so divine.

He soon returned to the USA.
It was such an exciting, fantastic day.
"You're home at last," M.J. let out a cry.
And now I must bid you all good-bye.

My story is now at its happy end.
I hope you enjoyed meeting my friend.

Sarah J. Nachin

Clyde's Scrapbook

*Andy Panda, Snowflake, Fergus & Me
at the New Curiosity Shop*

The Odyssey of Clyde the Camel

A neat sundial at St. Michael's Mount

Stonehenge — a weird bunch of rocks

The Odyssey of Clyde the Camel

Claudine, Pierre and me

Going on a hike in Andorra

A cool sculpture in Ordino, Andorra

The Odyssey of Clyde the Camel

Andorra – A fairy tale land

Sarah J. Nachin

*Jason "clowning around"
at the Cirque du Soleil*

The Odyssey of Clyde the Camel

The Cirque du Soleil

Sarah J. Nachin

The Barcelona Aquarium

The Odyssey of Clyde the Camel

*Beautiful stained-glass windows
at the Sagrada Familia*

Mural at the Parc de la Ciutadella

British English/American English Dictionary

ace - impressive
bee's knees - excellent
bloody - a mild curse word
brilliant - great, awesome
Brit - British people
chap - man
charity shop - thrift store
cheeky - impudent, bratty
cheers - short for "Cheerio" (good-bye)
chips - French fries
chum - friend
cooker - stove
crisps - potato chips
cuppa - cup of tea
estate agent - someone who sells real estate
Jerry - World War II German soldier
lift - elevator
limey - slang for an English person
loo - bathroom
luv – colloquialism for honey or dear
luvely - lovely
mobile - cell phone
motorway - freeway
Mum - Mom
ploughman's lunch - a meal made up of bread, cheese and pickled onions
pram - baby carriage
pub - bar that also serves meals

queue - a line you stand in
reception - front desk of a hotel
ring up - call someone on the telephone
salon - living room
scone - small, slightly sweet biscuit
solicitor - lawyer
ta-ta - slang for good-bye
telly - television
tube - subway in London
underground - subway
yank - an American

The Odyssey of Clyde the Camel

Index of People, Places, & Things

- **#10 Downing Street** – home of the British prime minister
- **95th Bomb Group** - https://www.facebook.com/groups/95thBG/
- **Ambassadors Theatre** - https://www.theambassadorstheatre.co.uk/Online/
- **Andorra** - a very small country located between France and Spain
- **Andorra la Vella** - the capital of Andorra
- **Anglican** - a Christian religion in England, also known as the Church of England
- **Aquarium Tropical des Pyrenees** - http://www.aquarium-tropical-pierrefitte.com/
- **Arc de Triomphe** - a large monument in Paris honoring French soldiers
- **Archbishop of Canterbury** - the leader of the Church of England
- **Barcelona** - a large city in Spain
- **Barcelona Aquarium** - https://www.aquariumbcn.com/en/
- **Bastille** - once a jail where prisoners were kept during the French Revolution
- **Bayswater Inn** - https://www.bayswaterinnhotel.com/
- **Brit Rail Pass** - discounted train tickets used in the United Kingdom
- **British Museum** - http://www.britishmuseum.org/
- **Buckingham Palace** - one of the palaces in London in which the English monarch resides

- **Calais** - a seaport on the northern coast of France
- **Catalan** - a language spoken in Andorra and parts of Spain
- **Clan Carakol Compañia** - https:www.facebook.com/clancarakol.compania
- **Cirque du Soleil** - https://www.cirquedusoleil.com/
- **Cornish pasties** - small meat and vegetable pies
- **Cornwall** - a region of England located on the west coast
- **Del Mar Hotel** - http://www.hoteldelmarbarcelona.com/
- **Doc Martin** - https://en.wikipedia.org/wiki/Doc_Martin
- **Dover** - a seaport on the southern coast of England
- **Èco Relais Hotel** - http://www.hotel-ecorelaispau.com/accueil/
- **English Channel** - a body of water separating England and France
- **Exincourt** - a town in the eastern part of France
- **Eye** - a small village in England
- **Felixstowe** - a town on the eastern seacoast of England
- **Fire Engine Inn** - http://thefireenginemarazion.pub/
- **Gare de Lyon** - a train station in Paris
- **Ger** - a small village in the southwestern part of France
- **Grottes de Betharram** - http://www.betharram.com/
- **Harrods Department Store** – https://www.harrods.com/en-gb
- **Horham** - a restored American Army Air Corps base used during World War II
- **Hotel Santa Barbara de la Vall d'Ordino** - http://hotelstabarbara.com/
- **Hyde Park** - a large park in London

The Odyssey of Clyde the Camel

- **Kensington Gardens** - a park in London and a residential neighborhood
- **Lawrence of Arabia** - an epic film based on the life of Thomas E. Lawrence, a British archaeologist, military officer, diplomat, and writer. He was renowned for his liaison role during the Sinai/Palestine Campaign and the Arab Revolt against the Ottoman Empire during WWI.
- **Magna Carta** - a document dating back to the 1200's, similar to the United States Constitution
- **Marazion** - a town in Cornwall on the western coast of England
- **Marlborough Hotel** –
- http://www.marlborough-hotel-felix.com/
- **Montbeliard** - a town in the eastern part of France
- **Montmartre** - a district in Paris
- **Montpellier** - a town in the southern part of France
- **Morris Mini** - a make of car that was manufactured in England at one time
- **Moulin Rouge** - http://www.moulinrouge.fr/?lang=en
- **Museu Picasso** - http://www.museupicasso.bcn.cat/en/
- **National Portrait Gallery** - http://www.npg.org.uk/
- **North Sea** - a large body of water bordering England and several other countries
- **Ordino** - a town in Andorra
- **Paddington Station** - a large train station in London
- **Parc de la Ciutadella** - http://www.barcelonaturisme.com/wv3/en/page/380/parc-dela-ciutadella.html
- **Pau** - a town in the southwestern part of France
- **Penzance** - a town in the Cornwall region of England

- **Père Lachaise Cemetery** - http://www.perelachaisecemetery.com/
- **Peugeot** - a make of car manufactured in France
- **Peugeot Museum** - http://www.musepeugeot.com/en/home.html
- **Piccadilly Circus** - a major traffic intersection in the West End of London
- **Pyrénées Mountains** - a mountain range that borders France and Spain
- **Rosetta Stone** - a rock containing carvings of the same text in 3 different languages. It proved to be the key to deciphering Egyptian hieroglyphs.
- **Sacré Coeur** - http://www.sacre-coeur-montmartre.com/english
- **Sagrada Familia** - http://www.sagradafamilia.org/
- **Salisbury Cathedral** - https://www.salisburycathedral.org.uk/
- **Sochaux** - a small town in the eastern part of France
- **Spa Pavilion** - https://spapavilion.uk/
- **St. Michael's Mount** - https://www.stmichaelsmount.co.uk/
- **Stonehenge** - http://www.english-heritage.org.uk/visit/places/stonehenge/
- **Take Time for Travel** - http://taketimefortravel.com/
- **The Desert Song** - an operetta that takes place in the deserts of Morocco
- **The Pirates of Penzance** - a comic opera about a fictional band of pirates
- **Toulouse** - a town in the southern part of France
- **Toulouse Museum** - https://www.museum.toulouse.fr/

- **Tower of London** - https://www.hrp.org.uk/tower-of-london/#gs.Q1GCpZ0
- **Trafalgar Square -** a large public square in central London
- **Tweedledee & Tweedledum** - characters in Alice in Wonderland who were twins
- **West End** - the theater district in London
- **Wheal Rodney Lodges** - http://www.whealrodney.co.uk/

About the Author

The Odyssey of Clyde the Camel is Sarah J. Nachin's third full-length published work. It is based on fact with some embellishment for entertainment purposes.

Sarah is a "jack of many trades" and she hopes a "master of some." Besides writing, her other passions are travel, photography and videography.

Sarah divides her time between her cottage in the Catskill Mountains and her home in Spring Hill, Florida. Her husband, Johnny Spinoso is her biggest fan and most trusted critic. He keeps her grounded in the real world.

For more information on Sarah go to her Facebook pages: Sarah Nachin and Sarah J. Nachin, Author.

Be sure and check out Nachin's other books:

ORDINARY HEROES, ANECDOTES OF VETERANS

Ordinary Heroes relates, in their own words, the experiences of men and women who served in the American military forces through five decades of conflict. These stories - humorous, heartwarming, tragic and gripping - are a testimony to the unconquerable human spirit.

THE LONG JOURNEY
with Felicia McCranie

THE LONG JOURNEY is the story of how one woman was saved from despair and self-destruction – the lowest place a person can be. She is now an ordained minister and shares her story to help other people find meaning and joy in their lives.

Both books are available on Amazon

www.ingramcontent.com/pod-product-compliance
Lightning Source LLC
Chambersburg PA
CBHW071515040426
42444CB00008B/1663